The K Chronicles

The Shaping of a Legend

Dennis Marksbury

ISBN:
979-8-9948452-0-2
First Printing Edition 2026

Cover design by Thomas Smith

TheKChronicles.com

TABLE OF CONTENTS

Dedication

From all of us who watched with wide eyes and pounding hearts.

To the man who didn't just take the mound, he owned it. Who brought the heat like a Texas summer, who made hitters guess, umpires flinch, and crowds erupt.

You were the headline, the highlight, the must-see moment. You turned strikeouts into spectacle, No-hitters into legend, and the fastball into fear itself.

You didn't pitch for the applause; you pitched because you *had to*. Because it was in your blood, your bones, your soul. And when the lights were brightest, you were electric.

From Shea to the Astrodome, from Anaheim to Arlington. You didn't just wear the uniform; you made it matter. You stood tall, threw hard, and never backed down.

So here's to *The Ryan Express,* To the man who left batters frozen, Fans breathless, And history rewritten.

For every K, every roar, every blister, every battle. For the seven no-hitters, the 5,714 strikeouts, the 27 seasons of fire, we tip our caps.

You were more than a pitcher. You were a force. A fury. A flamethrower with a heartbeat.

This one's for you, Nolan, from the kids who copied your windup, the dads who told stories about your stare, and the game that will never, ever forget your name.

— Your fans.

With Gratitude

To Steve Fernandez, a true Nolan Ryan fan and one of the most dedicated collectors in the world. Your knowledge and passion for Ryan's career are unmatched, and this book would not exist without you. That night, you looked over my milestones collection and said, "This would make a great book." You set something in motion that I never could have imagined. I am forever grateful for that spark.

To Ryan Guina, thank you for the many hours spent discussing, reviewing, and shaping this project. From draft chapters to long conversations and fresh ideas, your deep knowledge of baseball — and of Nolan Ryan's career in particular — added clarity and historical grounding at every step. Your careful proofreading sharpened the work, while your enthusiasm as a fellow Ryan collector added both depth and direction along the way.

To both of you, thank you. This book is as much yours as it is mine.

Introduction

Baseball is often remembered through the lens of individual greatness, record-breaking achievements, milestone moments, and the names that become immortalized in the game's annals. Nolan Ryan stands among the giants of baseball history, a pitcher whose dominance spanned four decades, whose fastball defied time, and whose records seem untouchable. But baseball is not played in solitude, and Ryan's career was not shaped in a vacuum. His legacy is not merely his own; it is also the story of the players who stood in the batter's box, the teammates who took the field beside him, and the countless individuals who played a role in his journey.

From the moment Ryan first stepped onto a Major League mound in 1966, his career became intertwined with those around him. The hitters who challenged him, the catchers who framed his fiery fastballs, the umpires who called his pitches, and the managers who made critical decisions each left an imprint on the career of the man who would become the all-time strikeout king. His milestones were not achieved alone. Every one of his 5,714 strikeouts had a name attached to it, each no-hitter required masterful defense behind him, and every record he set was a shared experience with those who played the game alongside him.

This book is not just about Nolan Ryan; it is about the people who helped define his career, the players who found themselves caught in the wake of his dominance, and those who, in turn, left a mark on him. Some names are legendary, Hall of Famers who squared off against him in unforgettable battles.

Others are lesser known, their names appearing only briefly in baseball's vast history books, yet forever linked to Ryan in a moment of triumph or heartbreak. These are the players who became part of his story, whether by striking out in a milestone moment, breaking up a no-hitter, or standing beside him in a dugout, witnessing history unfold.

Take, for example, César Gerónimo, the man who became Ryan's 3,000th strikeout victim. A talented outfielder in his own right, Gerónimo had already experienced the sting of history once before, having also been Bob Gibson's 3,000th strikeout. Then there's Robin Ventura, whose infamous charge to the mound in 1993 became one of the most replayed fights in baseball history, cementing both men's legacies in an instant of raw emotion and competitive fire.

And let's not forget the countless other players, rookies and veterans, All-Stars and journeymen who stepped into the batter's box and found themselves a part of history, whether they wanted to be or not.

Baseball is a game of connections, a tapestry woven together by shared experiences.

Ryan may have been the headliner, but this book seeks to tell the full story, one that includes the men who shaped his career as much as he shaped theirs. It is a collection of moments, each bound together by the common thread of Nolan Ryan's journey, told through the eyes of those who stood on the other side of the plate. This is not just a book about Nolan Ryan; it is a book about the game itself and the players who make it unforgettable.

Many of the stories in this book are built from firsthand interviews, personal correspondence, and public records. To preserve these voices and offer greater context, selected transcripts, extended quotes, and background materials are available at www.TheKChronicles.com. These supplemental resources offer a deeper look into the people and moments that helped shape Nolan Ryan's extraordinary journey.

Part I: Origins

Every legend has an origin story. Nolan Ryan's journey from a Texas teenager with a rocket arm to a major league phenom didn't happen by chance; it was shaped by early scouts, small moments of triumph, and the spark of something unmistakably special. This section captures the humble beginnings that ignited a career like no other.

Red Murff: The Scout Who Discovered a Legend

In 1965, while scouting in Alvin, Texas, Red Murff, a young scout for the New York Mets, found himself at the local high school watching a game that would change the course of baseball history. The 18-year-old Nolan Ryan, a skinny pitcher with a fiery arm, was on the mound. At first glance, Ryan didn't appear to have the physical build of a future Hall of Famer. He was slender, standing at just 6 feet 2 inches and weighing about 170 pounds. But Murf quickly noticed something extraordinary: the raw power behind Ryan's fastball. It wasn't just the speed, but the way Ryan's ball seemed to explode out of his hand with almost unreal velocity.

Red Murff was captivated. In an era when scouts often prioritized a pitcher's build and mechanics over raw stuff, Ryan's blazing fastball was undeniable.

Murf, who had scouted for several years, immediately saw the potential. He later recalled that Ryan had "the best arm I'd ever seen," and despite his lack of polish, Murf believed Ryan could make an impact at the major league level.

Against the standard of the time, Murf advocated strongly for the Mets to take a chance on Ryan, pushing for him to be drafted despite his unrefined pitching. Ryan's impressive stuff, along with his potential, convinced Murf that he had found a future star. In the 12th round of the 1965 MLB Draft, the Mets took a chance and selected Ryan. It wasn't an immediate payoff. Ryan was raw, often struggling with control, but Murf's discovery laid the foundation for what would become one of the most legendary pitching careers in baseball history.

Though Ryan would later be traded to the California Angels, he would go on to become a household name, setting records, tossing no-hitters, and becoming the face of pitching excellence for decades to come. But it all started with a scout who saw something in a young pitcher from

Alvin, Texas, whose potential was as big as his fastball. Red Murff's keen eye for talent and belief in Nolan Ryan set the stage for a career that would change the game forever.

Nolan Ryan: Learning in the Shadows

By the start of the 1969 season, Nolan Ryan had already spent parts of two years in the big leagues, but his place on the New York Mets' pitching staff was still uncertain. At just 22 years old, he was seen less as a foundational piece and more as a raw, high-risk arm — a power pitcher with electric stuff, yes, but control that came and went without warning. That season, he appeared in 25 games, but only 10 of them were starts. He worked mostly out of the bullpen, often entering games after the team's front-line arms had done the heavy lifting.

It was a staff stacked with talent, and Ryan was learning in the shadows of two rising stars.

The New York Mets' pitching staff stood at the crossroads of destiny and dominance. At its center was a young phenom named Tom Seaver — just 24 years old, but already the face of the franchise. Calm, cerebral, and surgical on the mound, Seaver led the Mets to 100 wins with a 25–7 record, a 2.21 ERA, and 208 strikeouts. He captured the National League Cy Young Award and finished second in the NL MVP voting.

Seaver had already won NL Rookie of the Year in 1967, and by the end of 1969, he had been selected to the All-Star team in each of his first three seasons. He would go on to appear in 12 All-Star Games, including seven straight from 1967 through 1973, and collect additional Cy Young Awards in 1973 and 1975. But in 1969, he was already The Franchise.

Alongside him stood Jerry Koosman, the quiet lefty who served as the perfect counterbalance. Koosman had finished runner-up for NL Rookie of the Year in 1968 and was an All-Star in both 1968 and 1969. He won 17 games that season and delivered key postseason performances, pitching with the kind of poise and command that anchored the Mets' staff when the stakes were highest.

While Seaver carried the aura of a franchise savior, it was Koosman who delivered the game-to-game stability that winning teams are built upon. He pitched brilliantly in Game 2 of the World Series, carrying the Mets to within one out of victory with 8⅔ commanding innings before Ron Taylor secured the final out, evening the series after an opening loss. And in Game 5, with a championship on the line, it was Koosman who got the ball—and the win—clinching the title with 9 gritty innings.

In many ways, Koosman's performances set the stage for Ryan's opportunity. By eating innings, controlling the damage, and keeping the Mets in command of the series, Koosman gave manager Gil Hodges the flexibility to use Ryan not as a developmental project, but as a weapon—an unburdened arm ready to be unleashed.

And then there was Ryan — the fireballer from Texas, still learning to tame his gift. His 92 strikeouts in just 89.1 innings hinted at the dominance to come, but his 53 walks were a reminder that he was a work in progress.

Yet in the chaos of postseason baseball, Hodges saw something in Ryan — not a future legend, but a threat.

Ryan pitched in two games during the National League Championship Series against Atlanta, contributing key relief innings as the Mets secured their trip to the World Series. And in Game 3 of the World Series against the heavily favored Baltimore Orioles, with the series tied 1–1, Gary Gentry carried a four-run lead into the seventh before Hodges handed the ball to Ryan. He closed the door with calm authority, protecting the advantage and delivering a pivotal save that pushed the Mets ahead in the series.

It was a turning point.

Ryan delivered 2⅓ scoreless innings, allowing just a single hit — a single by Clay Dalrymple — and striking out one. He held the Orioles in check and preserved the win for Gentry. It was the only World Series appearance of Ryan's career, and his only postseason save in 27 years of major league baseball.

That night, on baseball's biggest stage, Nolan Ryan stepped out from behind Seaver and Koosman, not to replace them, but to join them — if only briefly — in October glory.

Seaver and Koosman did not shape Nolan Ryan by instruction or imitation. They shaped him by presence. In a rotation anchored by certainty and command, Ryan was allowed to be exactly what he was — raw, explosive, imperfect. Seaver showed him what dominance looked like when harnessed. Koosman showed him how value could be built inning by inning. Together, they created the rarest gift for a young power pitcher: the freedom to fail without consequence, and the opportunity to succeed without fear.

Yet for collectors and fans, one thing already tied them together: their shared 1968 rookie card, printed before either had thrown a postseason pitch. One a right-handed flame thrower from Texas, the other a composed southpaw from

Minnesota. Their paths had not yet diverged. In 1969, they stood side by side — cardboard partners in a championship season, lifted together into baseball's brightest spotlight.

Part 2: Milestone Strikeouts

Thousands of milestones mark Ryan's career. This section tracks the strikeouts that marked history, showcasing some of the batters who became part of his legacy and the growing legend with each record-setting K.

Pat Jarvis: The First to Fall

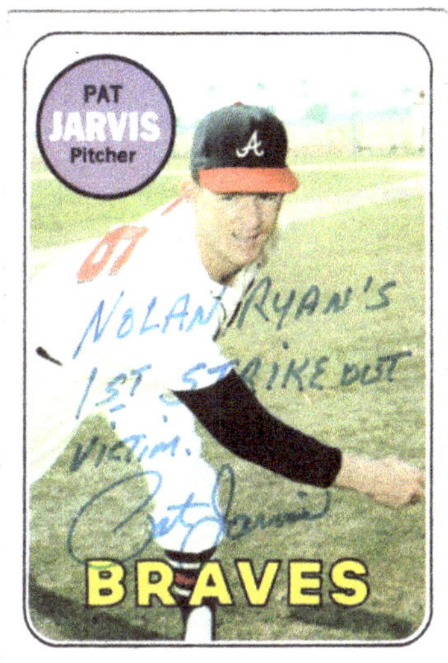

Before Nolan Ryan became a legend, known for no-hitters, 5,000 strikeouts, and awe-struck hitters, there was Pat Jarvis. On September 11, 1966, Jarvis, a young pitcher for the Atlanta Braves, stepped into the batter's box at Shea Stadium and, unknowingly, into baseball history. He would become the answer to a trivia question, a footnote in a Hall of Fame career, but more than that, he was the first name in a record book like no other.

Jarvis himself was in the early stages of his big league journey. Nicknamed "The Little Bulldog" for his tenacity, he had earned a spot in Atlanta's rotation after a strong showing in the minors. Though he would go on to carve out a respectable career, winning 85 games and pitching in two postseason series, his most enduring contribution to the game came not from the mound, but from one trip to the plate against a wiry 19-year-old Mets reliever making his Major League debut.

That reliever was Nolan Ryan.

Ryan’s arrival in the big leagues came with little fanfare. He wasn’t yet the mythic fireballer who would terrify generations of hitters.

He was just a teenager with a life ahead of him and something to prove. But in that moment, his first appearance in a New York Mets uniform, he showed the world what was to come. Jarvis was the first to fall, the first strikeout of Ryan’s Major League career.

Years later, after Ryan notched his 5,000th strikeout, reporters came calling. They wanted to hear from the man who had faced him first, to find out what it was like. Jarvis, never one to take himself too seriously, offered a reply as memorable as the milestone itself: **“My heart was in the game, but my ass was in the dugout. He threw me three straight fastballs, and I was glad to strike out.”**

That strikeout, mundane on its own, became the first domino in a chain of 5,714, a number so staggering it still looms over the sport like a monument.

It's hard to imagine in the moment how history is being made, but in hindsight, that encounter between two young pitchers was the starting point of a story that would come to define pitching dominance.

Pat Jarvis may not have known what he was stepping into that day, but his name is forever etched at the beginning of one of baseball's greatest legacies. For Nolan Ryan, it all began with a single pitch and with Pat Jarvis, the first to fall.

Sal Bando: The Captain at One Thousand

By the summer of 1973, Nolan Ryan was no longer a rising talent; he was a force gathering momentum. Pitching for the California Angels, he was in the midst of a season that would leave hitters unsettled and records reconsidered. On July 3 at the Oakland Coliseum, he reached a number that had long separated the exceptional from the ordinary — career strikeout number 1,000.

The man standing in was Sal Bando.

Bando was no ordinary opponent. The third baseman and captain of the defending World Series champion Oakland A's, he was the quiet center of one of baseball's most formidable clubs. His game was built on discipline and balance, on an understanding of the strike zone and the rhythm of an at-bat. From 1972 through 1974, he helped guide the A's to three straight championships, a dynasty defined not by flash, but by resolve.

And unlike many who faced Ryan in those years, Bando did not flinch.

Over the course of their careers, Bando saw Ryan 42 times at the plate. He collected ten hits in thirty-six official at-bats — a .278 average, better than his career mark and evidence that he was not overmatched by velocity alone. He knew how to wait. He knew how to survive. Against a pitcher who overwhelmed so many, Bando held his ground.

But baseball does not always belong to patterns. Sometimes it belongs to moments.

On that July afternoon, with the count leaning Ryan's way, the Angels' right-hander reached back and delivered the pitch that had come to define him. The fastball arrived late and hard. Bando swung — and missed. Strike three.

It was not a reckoning, and it was not a humiliation. It was a single pitch, placed at the right time, against a hitter who understood exactly what was coming. With it, Nolan Ryan became just the 20th pitcher in Major League history to reach 1,000 strikeouts — and one of the fastest to do so, still early in his career as a full-time starter.

The milestone did not diminish Bando's resistance. If anything, it underscored the truth of Ryan's ascent. Even those who could stand in against him, who could meet his speed with patience and poise, were never immune to the moment when his power took over.

The battles between the A's and the Angels were never just about individual lines in a box score. Oakland ruled the American League West with confidence and swagger. California chased from below, led by a pitcher whose presence alone altered the shape of a game. When they met, it was not dominance that defined the matchup — it was tension.

Ryan's 1,000th strikeout was not a warning shot aimed at weakness. It was a reminder that greatness does not require submission, only opportunity. Against a captain who rarely gave in, Nolan Ryan found his moment — and claimed it.

For Sal Bando, it became a single line in a long and accomplished career. For Nolan Ryan, it marked another step in a journey that would soon leave the numbers behind and enter the realm of legend.

SAL BANDO

MATCHUP SNAPSHOT

	PA	H	HR	BB	SO	AVG
vs. NOLAN RYAN	36	10	2	5	6	0.278
CAREER	8,208	1,790	242	1,031	923	0.254

Ron LeFlore: The Milestone That Almost Wasn't

By the summer of 1976, Nolan Ryan was no longer just a promising young fireballer; he was a pitcher entering rarefied air. On August 31, pitching for the California Angels against the Detroit Tigers, Ryan stood on the brink of another milestone. With one more strikeout, he would join a small and exclusive group of pitchers with 2,000 career strikeouts.

Stepping to the plate was Detroit's electrifying leadoff man, Ron LeFlore, a player whose path to the big leagues was as improbable as any in baseball history. Not long before his debut, LeFlore's talent was discovered in one of the unlikeliest of places, a difficult chapter of his life that made his ascent all the more remarkable. Now, he was the Tigers' everyday center fielder, known for his blazing speed, fearless approach, and relentless energy.

LeFlore didn't just run, he disrupted, turning singles into doubles and stolen bases into momentum shifts. In 1976, he was in the midst of a breakout season, piling up 212 hits, 93 runs scored, and 58 stolen bases.

But that night in Anaheim, even his quick bat couldn't match Ryan's overpowering arsenal.

With one of his signature fastballs, Ryan fanned LeFlore for career strikeout number 2,000.

The moment carried extra weight given LeFlore's reputation. He wasn't an easy out. In fact, over his career, LeFlore posted a respectable .288 batting average, with 1,283 hits and 455 stolen bases across nine seasons. Specifically, against Ryan, the dynamic shifted. LeFlore managed just a .200 average (9 hits in 45 at-bats) with 22 strikeouts, a testament to how even the league's most aggressive hitters often struggled against Ryan's overpowering mix of heat and movement.

This wasn't the last time they would face each other. Ryan and LeFlore's careers intersected throughout the late '70s and early '80s, a constant test of power versus speed, fire versus finesse. Their matchups became a quiet footnote in Ryan's steady climb through baseball's record books.

But on that August night in 1976, with one swing and a miss, Ron LeFlore became part of history. For him, it was a fleeting strikeout in a career defined by improbable opportunity. For Nolan Ryan, it was another step toward greatness, a reminder that his blistering fastball wasn't just a spectacle; it was rewriting the standards of what a pitcher could be.

And the climb was far from over.

RON LEFLORE

MATCHUP SNAPSHOT

	PA	H	HR	BB	SO	AVG
vs. NOLAN RYAN	49	9	0	4	22	0.200
CAREER	4,872	1,283	59	363	888	0.288

Cesar Geronimo: Gloved Greatness, Struck by Fire

On a scorching Fourth of July afternoon in Cincinnati, Nolan Ryan did what he always seemed to do: he threw a fastball past a Major League hitter. But this one was different. When César Gerónimo stood frozen at the plate, called out on strikes in the third inning at Riverfront Stadium, he became a permanent part of baseball history.

And Gerónimo was no easy out.

A two-time World Series champion, four-time Gold Glove winner, and a steady fixture in center field for the Big Red Machine, Gerónimo wasn't a hitter pitchers circled for strikeouts. Over a 15-year career, he batted .258 with 977 hits, 51 home runs, 82 stolen bases, and a reputation built more on defense, speed, and discipline than power.

His glove patrolled the spacious outfields of Riverfront Stadium, and his cool, steady presence made him a valued piece of Cincinnati's dynasty.

But against Nolan Ryan, nobody was safe.

Over their matchups, Gerónimo managed one hit in 6 at-bats, a .167 average, but Ryan got him three times on strikes, the most memorable coming on that blistering summer afternoon. That third-inning punchout was Ryan's 3,000th career strikeout, vaulting him into one of baseball's most exclusive clubs.

At the time, only three men had done it: Walter Johnson, Bob Gibson, and Gaylord Perry. Each reached the milestone with their own unique brand of greatness: Johnson with unmatched dominance, Gibson with searing intensity, and Perry with crafty deception and a not-so-secret reputation for bending the rules.

Ryan, though, did it with raw, unrelenting velocity.

In typical fashion, he didn't celebrate. He walked off the mound, head down, laser-focused on the next batter. There was still a game to play, though the Astros would go on to lose 8–1.

But the story didn't end there for Gerónimo. Years earlier, in another chapter of baseball history, he had also been Bob Gibson's 3,000th strikeout victim, making him the only player ever to wear that unusual badge twice struck out for milestone Ks by two of the most feared arms the game has ever known.

Gerónimo took it all in stride. Quiet, steady, and always a professional, he wore the odd piece of trivia with pride.

That was the magic of July 4, 1980, not the fireworks, not the final score, but the moment frozen in time when Nolan Ryan joined the legends, and César Gerónimo, for the second time, became the face of history.

CESAR GERONIMO

MATCHUP SNAPSHOT

	PA	H	HR	BB	SO	AVG
vs. NOLAN RYAN	8	1	0	2	3	0.167
CAREER	3,780	977	51	354	746	0.258

Danny Heep: In the Path of a Legend

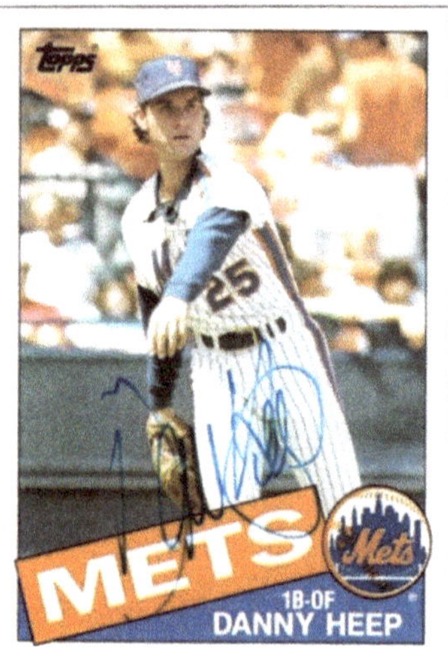

On July 11, 1985, beneath the glowing roof of the Houston Astrodome, Nolan Ryan reached a milestone never before achieved in Major League Baseball. In the sixth inning of a game against the New York Mets, he struck out outfielder Danny Heep for his 4,000th career strikeout, a staggering, unprecedented mark in the sport's long history.

Heep, a left-handed hitter and former Astro, had spent parts of three seasons with Houston before being traded to New York in 1982.

Known for his versatility in the outfield and his steady presence off the bench, Heep had carved out a role as a reliable contributor, even if he wasn't a household name. On this night, batting sixth for the Mets, he led off the inning against Ryan, a man he once called a teammate.

The count quickly ran to 0–2. Then came a sharp curveball in the dirt. Heep swung over it, and the Astrodome crowd erupted in recognition. Flashbulbs popped, teammates rushed toward Ryan, and history added another entry to its endless ledger.

The strikeout was more than just a number. It marked Ryan as the first pitcher to reach 4,000, a testament to the longevity, ferocity, and dominance that defined his career. He had already passed Walter Johnson and Gaylord Perry on the all-time list and now stood alone in uncharted territory. At 38 years old, Ryan was still overpowering hitters with the same explosive fastball and sharp breaking ball that had marked his earlier years in New York and California.

The game itself reflected the intensity of the moment, a 4–3 Astros win that stretched into extra innings.

Ryan pitched seven strong innings, struck out eleven, and allowed just one earned run. His performance was vintage Nolan Ryan: precise, punishing, and relentless.

For Heep, the moment became an unlikely landmark in his own journey. Although never a star, he built a respectable career, batting .257 across 13 Major League seasons, contributing to postseason teams with the Mets and

Dodgers, and proving his value as a reliable left-handed bat off the bench. Heep finished with 503 career hits, 30 home runs, and 229 RBIs, a modest but meaningful tenure at baseball's highest level.

And unlike many, Heep had his moments against Ryan. Over his career, he faced the fireballer 41 times (plate appearances) and collected 10 hits for a .263 average, including a home run. But on that humid July night in Houston, Ryan got the better of him, adding Heep's name to the long, humbling list of hitters who couldn't solve the riddle of Ryan's arsenal.

But for all the strikeouts, for all the legends who fell victim to Ryan's fastball, it was fitting, almost poetic, that a former teammate, a quiet grinder like Danny Heep, stood in the box when Nolan Ryan made history once again.

In the vast story of Ryan's singular career, Heep became another name etched into the long shadow cast by 60 feet and 6 inches.

DANNY HEEP

MATCHUP SNAPSHOT	PA	H	HR	BB	SO	AVG
vs. NOLAN RYAN	41	10	1	2	6	0.263
CAREER	2,222	503	30	220	242	0.257

Rickey Henderson: Where Legends Collide

Rickey Henderson, often regarded as the greatest leadoff hitter in baseball history, was known for his speed, on-base ability, and knack for stealing bases. With 1,406 stolen bases and numerous records to his name, Henderson's influence on the game was undeniable. His involvement in Nolan Ryan's 5,000th career strikeout further cemented both players' legacies in baseball history.

Henderson's career spanned from 1979 to 2003, during which he became a 10-time All-Star, the all-time leader in stolen bases, and carried a career batting average of .279.

His ability to disrupt games and change their course with his speed made him one of the most feared players in the league. But on August 22, 1989, Henderson became part of an even more significant milestone in Nolan Ryan's storied career.

That night, during a game between Ryan's Texas Rangers and Henderson's Oakland Athletics, Ryan reached his 5,000th career strikeout. In the top of the fifth inning, Ryan faced Henderson, who was leading off for the Athletics. With a fastball high in the strike zone, Ryan struck Henderson out, making history as the first pitcher ever to reach 5,000 strikeouts.

According to Walt McCreary, Henderson's longtime friend and confidant, Rickey knew exactly what was at stake when he stepped into the batter's box. "He admired greatness," McCreary said. "After the strikeout, he said, 'Man, how cool is that?'" For a man who prided himself on competing against the best, there was no shame in falling to Ryan only respect. "You're part of history," McCreary recalled him saying. "And it... I don't even know if Rickey even tried to make contact with the ball that damn game."

The moment was special not only because of Ryan's achievement but also because of Henderson's stature as one of the game's premier leadoff hitters. But even with all his speed, discipline, and instincts, Henderson had struggled against Ryan throughout their careers. In 17 official at-bats, he managed just two hits, a .118 average, and struck out five times. “Here you have a Hall of Famer like Rickey Henderson, 3,000-plus base hits,” McCreary said, “and facing another true Hall of Famer, and he made Rickey look like a minor leaguer.”

Rather than being frustrated, Henderson appreciated the historical weight of the moment. According to McCreary, Rickey even asked the catcher before stepping in if he could have the ball if he struck out. “The catcher told him to go f*** himself,” McCreary laughed, “but that was Rickey. Always a character.”

Behind the swagger and speed, Henderson was a true student of the game. “He didn’t need the front office to hand him analytics,” McCreary explained. “He studied the game himself. He kept little pieces of paper, wrote things down, remembered what pitchers had done. He lived it and lived for it.” And when facing the best pitchers, like Ryan, Henderson approached it with reverence.

“He’d make sure to get extra sleep,” McCreary said. “Because it’s the best facing the best. That’s what it comes down to.”

And while Henderson is best remembered by many for his stolen base records, he took greater pride in another, less flashy mark: the all-time runs scored record. “That was the one he really loved,” McCreary said. “He’d always say, ‘How do you win a game? By runs.’ And nobody crossed the plate more than he did.”

Rickey Henderson’s role in Nolan Ryan’s 5,000th strikeout serves as a reminder of their lasting impact on the game. Two titans, one on the mound, one at the plate, locked in a moment of mutual respect and history. As McCreary put it, “Those two had a lot of love for the game. It wasn’t about the money. They were gamers. They admired each other. And that strikeout… that was greatness meeting greatness.”

RICKEY HENDERSON

MATCHUP SNAPSHOT

	PA	H	HR	BB	SO	AVG
vs. NOLAN RYAN	22	2	0	5	5	0.118
CAREER	13,346	3,055	297	2,190	1,694	0.279

Greg Myers: The Final Flame

On September 17, 1993, in what would unknowingly become the final chapter in one of the most legendary careers in baseball history, Nolan Ryan stepped onto the mound at the Kingdome in Seattle. At 46 years old and in his 27th and final season, Ryan was nearing the end of a journey defined by power, dominance, and milestones no one had thought possible. And fittingly, even in his waning days, he still had one last piece of history to write.

In the bottom of the first inning, with two outs and a man on first, Ryan faced Mariners catcher Greg Myers. The veteran pitcher reared back and delivered one of his trademark fastballs, still blazing in the low 90s. Myers swung and missed strike three. It was career strikeout number 5,714, the final punch out of Nolan Ryan's unmatched total, a record that still towers over the rest of Major League Baseball.

The significance of the moment was not immediately apparent to those watching. No one knew it would be Ryan's last strikeout. But looking back, it was a poetic moment, the final K from a man whose entire career had been defined by strikeouts.

Greg Myers, a solid journeyman catcher, now holds a permanent place in baseball trivia lore as the answer to a question asked in every dugout: *"Who was Nolan Ryan's last strikeout?"*

A few days later, on September 22, Ryan would take the mound one last time in Arlington. But in that game, his arm gave out, a torn ligament mid-inning ended his career, not with a strikeout, but with a grimace and a walk off the field. And so, Myers' strikeout remained the final moment of Nolan Ryan's greatness in motion, the last time his fireball overwhelmed a batter.

There was no ceremony that day in Seattle, no standing ovation or grand farewell. But that simple swing-and-miss against Greg Myers now stands as the punctuation mark at the end of a Hall of Fame sentence, a perfect symbol of the career of a pitcher who defied age, logic, and limits for nearly three decades.

GREG MYERS

MATCHUP SNAPSHOT	PA	H	HR	BB	SO	AVG
vs. NOLAN RYAN	30	3	1	2	11	0.115
CAREER	3,362	776	87	268	539	0.255

Part 3: Record-Breaking Moments

Some moments didn't just build Ryan's legacy; they redefined what was possible in the game. This section highlights some of Ryan's most iconic achievements, complete with the pressure, the drama, and the players who were there when history was made.

Carried on the Air: The First No-Hitter

A hard wind carried through Royals Stadium that night, but it was Nolan Ryan's fastball that truly moved. It wasn't just quick—it climbed, late and heavy, like something trying to escape gravity. Batters didn't solve him. They barely touched him. And when they did, the ball rose.

Twelve men struck out, overmatched and outpaced. But that alone wasn't enough.

A no-hitter, after all, is never one man's accomplishment. It is a series of moments—some loud, most quiet—held together by precision and trust.

That night, the Kansas City Royals challenged Ryan not by squaring him up, but by lifting the ball, asking it to find grass. Three times, fly balls took flight with intent. And three times, Angels outfielders moved without panic. They ran the right routes, opened the glove at the right time, and answered without flourish. One ball at a time, the silence held.

Only once did the ball stay down. A hard grounder shot toward the middle, hot and true. The shortstop ranged left, fielded clean, and made the throw without delay. No applause, no drama. But a beat too late, and the story breaks. Instead, the inning moved on, intact.

By the eighth, everything was brittle. One misstep, one ball drifting too far, and the whole thing could vanish. Then came Rudy Meoli's play.

It wasn't heroic in the cinematic sense. It was more fragile than that—measured and exact. The ball carried deep into left-center, turning Meoli around. He ran with his back to the infield, tracked it over his shoulder, and closed his glove just before the moment passed. The kind of catch you don't appreciate until later, when you realize what never happened.

Still, even a masterpiece needs a final brushstroke.

In the ninth, rookie manager Bobby Winkles made his move. He summoned Ken Berry—a two-time Gold Glover, now watching from the bench. This wasn't about sentiment. It was about certainty.

With two outs, Steve Hovley lifted a high fly to the right-field corner. It hung just long enough to raise doubt. Berry turned, ran, and found the fence as the wind nudged the ball downward.

"They put me in for defense," Berry would recall. "I wasn't in the game until the ninth inning. It looked like it was going to be a play where I had to jump up on the fence, make the catch. The wind caught the ball and killed it. So I had gotten to the fence, I was able to stretch up a little bit, reach up and make the play. But I didn't have to jump. It was not a great, great play. It just happened to be a great time for the play to take place."

The glove closed. The game ended. The no-hitter stood.

It was the first of seven for Nolan Ryan—but this one came with help. From Berry's late entrance to Meoli's quiet turn, to every clean route and simple throw, the story was built on trust. On a night where everything seemed to rise, nothing was allowed to fall.

Nolan Ryan threw a no-hitter. But the Angels caught it.

Jeff Torborg: The Quiet Receiver of Thunder

Jeff Torborg never had the stats to jump off a page. A lifetime .214 hitter in a ten-year career with the Dodgers and Angels, he was the kind of player whose true value never showed up in box scores. But behind the plate, Torborg was steady, intelligent, and trusted especially by pitchers who had something special in their arms. By the time he joined the Angels in 1971, he had already caught no-hitters from two of the hardest-throwing right-handers of his generation: Sandy Koufax's perfect game in 1965 and Bill Singer's no-hitter in 1970. That kind of résumé doesn't happen by accident.

Koufax had power and command, Singer had raw fire, and Torborg handled both without fanfare. He had a knack for navigating pitchers through emotional innings and tight strike zones.

He framed without flourish, spoke in few words, and rarely visited the mound unless he had to. That kind of composure became his signature, and it would serve him well when he found himself catching a young Nolan Ryan in Anaheim.

Ryan was a unique project. Unlike Koufax or Singer, Ryan's stuff sometimes bordered on uncatchable. His fastball was already legendary, but his control could vanish without warning. In his first full season with the Angels in 1972, Ryan led the league in both strikeouts and walks, a contradiction that perfectly defined the chaos he carried to the mound.

Torborg saw the talent, of course. Everyone did. But what he also saw was a pitcher who needed space to grow and someone steady to guide him pitch by pitch. And yet, for all the violence in Ryan's delivery, Torborg brought a calming rhythm. He called games with purpose, slowed Ryan down when needed, and helped instill a sense of control in a pitcher known for being untamed.

When Ryan threw his first no-hitter on May 15, 1973, it was Torborg behind the plate, marking the third no-hitter Torborg had caught in his career. That milestone put him in a class all his own. At the time, no other catcher had caught no-hitters for three different pitchers.

And these weren't soft tossers or groundball artists; they were flame-throwers, the type who needed a catcher who wouldn't flinch.

But the no-hitter was just one night. Torborg's influence on Ryan was something deeper. In Ryan's early years in Anaheim, Torborg was a quiet mentor, a catcher who had seen greatness up close and knew how to guide it without ever claiming credit. Ryan would go on to throw six more no-hitters, but the first came with Torborg as his anchor.

When people talk about no-hitters, they talk about the pitcher. But in Torborg's case, his fingerprints are all over three of them: Koufax's brilliance, Singer's dominance, and Ryan's first glimpse of control within the storm. He didn't make headlines. He didn't ask for attention. But Jeff Torborg, in his quiet way, caught more than history. He caught lightning three times.

Rudy Meoli: The Unsung Hero of Ryan's No-Hitters

Rudy Meoli's name may not be the first that comes to mind when recalling Nolan Ryan's legendary no-hitters. Still, the versatile infielder played a quiet, crucial role in preserving history during multiple chapters of Ryan's early dominance. While the Ryan Express roared with strikeouts and heat, it was often the men behind him who ensured his brilliance translated into baseball immortality.

On May 15, 1973, during Ryan's first career no-hitter against the Kansas City Royals, Rudy Meoli was manning his usual position at shortstop. Late in the game, with two outs in the eighth inning and a runner on first, Royals hitter Gail Hopkins lifted a blooper into shallow left-center field.

Meoli turned and sprinted back, making a spectacular over-the-shoulder catch to end the inning and preserve the no-hitter heading into the final frame.

It was a defining defensive moment in a game dominated by Ryan's overpowering fastball.

Reflecting on that night, Meoli recalled not just the historic finish, but the surprising pregame ritual that may have helped set the tone:

> *"The first no-hitter in KC was amazing," Meoli said. "Nolan, Bill Singer, Rich Hand, and I went to a chiropractor on the first day in town. I think it really helped. Besides Nolan's no-hitter, I had my best career day batting during that series. Had to love playing with these guys and Frank Robinson."*

Photo courtesy of Rudy Meoli: Jimmie Reese conducting pregame fungo drills alongside #12 Winston Llenas and other California Angels players. Circa 1973 season.

Just two months later, on July 15, 1973, Meoli was back at his natural position, shortstop, for Ryan's second no-hitter of the season, this time against the Detroit Tigers. As the game wore on, a familiar feeling began to creep in. *"Not until the seventh inning,"* Meoli later said when asked if the team sensed history repeating itself. *"The stuff got better the longer he stayed on the mound.*

Like he was really loose and the rhythm was even better." With two outs in the ninth, Tigers slugger Norm Cash popped a weak fly toward the infield. Meoli drifted under it and squeezed his glove around the final out, sealing another piece of history.

But Meoli's time beside Ryan wasn't all triumph. On August 29, 1973, Ryan was again masterful, this time against the Yankees. In the first inning, Thurman Munson lifted a soft blooper between second and short. Meoli and Sandy Alomar both charged, but a split-second miscommunication allowed the ball to fall untouched, the only hit of the game. Instead of a third no-hitter, Ryan had to settle for a one-hit shutout.

Meoli later reflected on that moment with humility and a sense of humor: *"That day the ball dropped should have been ruled a team error. There I made a new stat!"*

Scan to visit KChronicles.com for more details!

Then came August 7, 1974, against the White Sox. Ryan was once again three outs from another no-hitter, and Meoli was manning third base, not his usual post. With none out in the ninth, Dick Allen hit a slow roller. Meoli charged, but Allen beat the throw by a blink. Ryan's bid for another no-no was gone.

Whether catching pop flies in right field, securing the final out at short, or being caught in near-misses that haunt no-hitter lore, Rudy Meoli was there, steadfast, unflashy, and essential. While Ryan's name dominates the headlines, Meoli's glove and grit were threaded into the fabric of those unforgettable nights.

Rich Reese: Caught in the Wake of Ryan's 383rd

On the evening of September 27, 1973, Anaheim Stadium became the backdrop for a seismic moment in baseball history. Nolan Ryan, already feared for his flamethrower fastball, entered the game against the Minnesota Twins needing 16 strikeouts to surpass Sandy Koufax's hallowed single-season record of 382. It was a tall order, but Ryan never did things the easy way.

As the game stretched into extra innings, Ryan's strikeout tally crept higher, inching toward history. One final batter stood between him and the record: Rich Reese.

At 35 years old, Reese was in the twilight of his career, serving as a reliable pinch hitter and veteran presence off the bench.

Over ten big-league seasons, mostly with the Minnesota Twins, Reese had carved out a steady role. He owned a career batting average of .253, with 52 home runs and 245 RBIs. Though never a superstar, he'd been part of postseason runs and had contributed to the Twins' 1969 division title. He was no stranger to Ryan, either; the two had faced off before, including earlier that night when Reese managed a double off the hard-throwing right-hander.

But fate has a way of choosing unlikely characters for the game's biggest chapters. In what would be his final at-bat in the major leagues, Reese became part of baseball immortality. His strikeout marked number 383 for Ryan, a new Major League Baseball record, surpassing Koufax's mark set eight years earlier.

What makes the moment all the more poignant is its finality. Reese, the steady veteran, never played another major league game. His last contribution wasn't a home run or a walk-off hit it was becoming the exclamation point on one of the most untouchable records in baseball.

Ryan finished the night with 16 strikeouts in an 11-inning complete game, earning both the victory and a place alone atop the record books.

But it’s the image of that final strikeout, the flash of heat past Rich Reese, that remains frozen in time.

Norm Cash: The Final Out and a Bit of Theater

One of the most dramatic and memorable moments in Nolan Ryan's career came during a game against the Detroit Tigers on July 15, 1973, when Ryan pitched his second no-hitter of the season. This historic performance, which helped solidify Ryan as one of baseball's most dominant forces, became even more unforgettable thanks to an unusual moment involving Tigers slugger Norm Cash.

Cash, known for his powerful swing and quirky personality, was the final batter Ryan faced that day. But when he stepped to the plate with two outs in the ninth inning, Cash traded his regular bat for something far more unconventional: a 36-inch table leg.

The oversized piece of lumber, intended as both a protest and a source of humor, became an iconic image from the game and a symbol of just how overpowering Ryan had been.

Ryan, unfazed by the theatrics, stayed locked in. He delivered his pitch, and Cash, swinging wildly with the table leg, struck out to end the game.

The sight of Cash's stunt only added to the legend of Ryan's no-hitter, a playful yet telling acknowledgment of Ryan's intimidating presence on the mound.

While Ryan's blistering fastball and 17 strikeouts were the true stars of the day, the moment with Cash provided a unique, lighthearted twist to an otherwise dominant performance. For Ryan, it marked his second no-hitter, both achieved within a remarkable two-month stretch, setting the stage for what would become a record-breaking seven no-hitters over his career.

Cash's antics didn't detract from the moment they enhanced it, turning an already historic game into one of the most unique chapters in baseball history. His final strikeout, table leg and all, ensured that this particular no-hitter would never be forgotten.

1983: The Summer of 3,509

1921 Senators Player Panel

For more than half a century, the summit of 3,508 strikeouts stood like a granite peak in baseball's mountainous record book. Walter Johnson had carved it into the game's highest elevations in 1927, and it remained there, untouched by time and progress. Through decades of flame-throwers and control artists, expansion eras and elevated mounds, The Big Train held firm. His mark, etched over 21 seasons with the Senators, was less a statistic than a sacred number, whispered with awe, not expectation.

But as the 1980s dawned, three men, each with his own style, temperament, and legacy, began a slow, dramatic climb toward Johnson's throne. Nolan Ryan, the stoic Texan with a lightning bolt for an arm. Steve Carlton, the silent master whose slider could vanish like breath on a mirror. And Gaylord Perry, the guileful veteran whose grip and grit had carried him through two decades of reinvention. Between them, they shared thousands of innings, countless confrontations, and a singular ambition: to become the greatest strikeout pitcher the game had ever seen.

Ryan was the first to arrive. On April 27, 1983, in the sterile dome of Olympic Stadium in Montreal, he stared down Brad Mills of the Expos in the bottom of the eighth inning. Mills, a reliable pinch-hitter that season, later recalled that he "had no idea there was a chance it was me." There was no official countdown on the scoreboard, no announcement from the press box, just another at-bat in another late-inning substitution. "We knew he only needed a few K's for the record," Mills said, "but there was no mention of any countdown on our bench or on the scoreboard."

The sequence unfolded quickly: a fastball for strike one, another fouled off 0-2. Then came the curveball. Mills held back. "The bench for the Astros jumped up, they thought it was strike three," he remembered. "That's when I knew I was it." He stepped out of the box, certain Ryan would finish the moment with his signature fastball. But instead, Ryan doubled down on the same breaking pitch. "He threw the same curveball I took for the third strike; it was outside as well," Mills said. "His team ran out of the dugout and mobbed him."

The crowd rose to its feet in a standing ovation. Teammates surrounded Ryan on the mound, the weight of history briefly giving way to the joy of achievement. In that instant, baseball's most enduring record, Walter Johnson's 3,508 strikeouts, had fallen.

Six weeks later, Steve Carlton joined him. On June 7, pitching for the Phillies against the Cardinals, he fanned Lonnie Smith to claim his share of the summit. There was less fanfare, fewer flashbulbs. Carlton, ever the recluse, didn't offer much in the way of reflection. He rarely did. He didn't need to. His presence on the mound was his voice silent, precise, and utterly dominant. While Ryan attacked with fury, Carlton dissected with elegance.

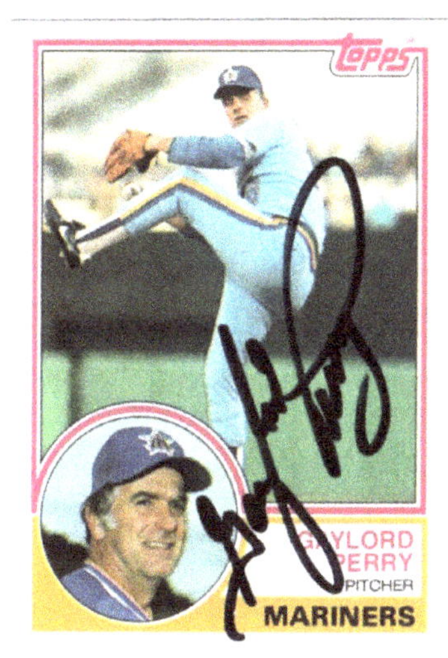

Then came Gaylord Perry. At 44 years old, with more than 300 wins and a thousand stories behind him, he was still spinning breaking balls for the Seattle Mariners. On August 13, 1983, against the Yankees, Perry struck out Steve Kemp to notch his 3,509th career strikeout, matching Walter Johnson's once-untouchable mark. For a brief, remarkable moment, three men stood side by side in the record books, each having scaled a peak untouched since the 1920s. Perry, often dismissed as a relic or sideshow, had made a career of outsmarting hitters and outlasting assumptions. Now, with that strikeout, he had etched his name alongside the legends.

But Perry's time in the chase was fleeting. By the time he reached Johnson's hallowed number, Ryan and Carlton had already pushed beyond it, turning the record into a two-person duel that captivated the game. Over the final months of the 1983 season, Ryan and Carlton took turns at the summit in one of the most compelling statistical chases in modern baseball.

From July through the end of the campaign, they repeatedly traded the lead. The margin between them was often razor-thin, sometimes fewer than five strikeouts. At one point, they stood in perfect deadlock. Neither man spoke publicly about the race, but the baseball world spoke plenty for them. Sports pages printed daily tallies. Television broadcasters tracked every appearance. Fans, scorecards in hand, began watching not just for wins or losses but for the lonely arc of a swinging third strike.

On July 19, Ryan overtook Carlton once more. Carlton regained the top spot in early August. Then, on August 22, Ryan threw a ten-strikeout gem to move back ahead. Nine days later, Carlton matched the feat, fanning ten on August 31 to reclaim the lead again. The baton passed like clockwork, each man responding to the other with performances that still shimmer in the scorebooks.

By season's end, it was Carlton who held the edge: 3,709 to Ryan's 3,677. Perry, whose brief brush with history had come and gone in under a month, retired shortly after with 3,534. His total, once historic, had become the floor of a record now being rewritten in real time.

In 1984, the race resumed, but now it tilted. Carlton, aging and mortal, began to fade. Ryan, still a storm in motion, closed the gap. The lead saw brief seesawing in spring, but the defining moment came on September 5 in San Diego. In the third inning, Ryan struck out Kevin McReynolds to reach 3,863 career strikeouts. With that, he passed Carlton for the final time.

The torch, after so many months had passed in silence between two men who never spoke of the race, would never pass again.

Carlton continued until 1988, retiring with 4,136 strikeouts. But it was Ryan who remained in motion, his arm still alive, his body still built for the grind. He pitched nine more seasons, struck out another 1,851 men, and retired in 1993 with 5,714 strikeouts, a number no one had dreamed of chasing. Yet the number alone was never the whole of the story. The chase itself, especially that breathless summer of 1983, was baseball at its most elemental: two legends on parallel tracks, pushing one another with every pitch, even from opposite coasts. When Ryan finally stood alone, it was only because he and Carlton had first walked side by side, step for step, to the gates of history.

Howe and Sierra: Anchors of the No-Hit Frame

Two of Nolan Ryan's most celebrated achievements, the fifth and sixth no-hitters of his career, were defined not only by his overpowering fastball but by the fielders who delivered the final out. While Ryan's legacy was written with strikeouts and dominance, it was the calm execution of his teammates that sealed the record books.

Art Howe: The Professor on the Field

Before he became a respected big-league manager, Art Howe built his name as a cerebral, versatile infielder with the Houston Astros.

A late bloomer by baseball standards, Howe didn't debut in the majors until age 27, having been signed out of the University of Wyoming and working his way up through the minors with quiet tenacity. What he lacked in flash, he made up for in poise and preparation. He played all four infield positions during his career, but it was his time at third base with the Astros in the late 1970s and early '80s that cemented his value.

Howe's strength was never about jaw-dropping stats. He brought steadiness to a team that often leaned on pitching and defense. Coaches trusted him. Teammates respected him. In a clubhouse filled with bigger personalities, Howe was the kind of player who made everyone better simply by knowing the game inside and out. His teammates called him "The Professor," a nod to both his glasses and his methodical, intelligent approach to the game.

In the winter following the 1979 season, the Astros made a move that altered the franchise's trajectory. "In '79, the year before we got Nolan, we had a big lead at the All-Star break. I thought we were finally going to win the division, but we ran out of gas and lost it to Cincinnati. That winter, we traded for Nolan, and that's when I knew we were serious. Our chances, as far as I was concerned, went through the roof."

Ryan's arrival brought instant credibility and renewed belief. "When he joined us, we all believed we could win. When he arrived at spring training, everyone went over to shake his hand. He didn't act like a superstar; he was just one of us.

A prankster, a good teammate. And his work ethic was off the charts."

That baseball intellect came into play on September 26, 1981, at the Astrodome, when Ryan was chasing his fifth no-hitter. With two outs in the ninth, Dusty Baker grounded a ball toward third. Howe, calm as ever, fielded it cleanly and fired it across the diamond to Denny Walling at first base. "He wasn't even there yet when I threw it like a quarterback leading a receiver," Howe recalled. "He turned around just in time and caught it. And that was the final out. The celebration began."

Though Howe had only seen one grounder all game, he was prepared for the moment. "First thought: get in front of it. If I didn't field it cleanly, I wanted it to be an error so the no-hitter stayed alive. Thankfully, I made the play." Years later, he reflected on the significance of that final out: "It was a thrill to be a part of that. Honestly, with all his one-hitters, he could've had 10 or 12 no-hitters."

Even years later, Howe remained proud of the trust Ryan had in him. "I think Nolan later said he was glad the ball was hit to me that he trusted I'd make the play. That meant a lot to me."

Ruben Sierra: El Caballo in Right Field

Ruben Sierra burst onto the major league scene in the mid-1980s like a bolt of electricity. A switch-hitting outfielder from Puerto Rico, Sierra signed with the Texas Rangers as a teenager and debuted at age 20 in 1986. He quickly became known for his whip-strong swing, his swagger, and his ability to hit for both power and average. In 1989, at just 23 years old, he led the American League in RBIs and triples, finished second in MVP voting, and established himself as one of the most exciting young players in the game.

To teammates and fans, he was *El Caballo*—**The Horse**—a nickname that reflected both his physical power and his relentless energy. While his bat made the headlines, Sierra's athleticism was always present. He played the outfield with confidence, armed with a cannon arm and a flair that could turn routine into spectacle.

That flair would come into play on June 11, 1990, when 43-year-old Nolan Ryan was facing the defending World Series champion Oakland A's, chasing history once more.

With two outs in the ninth inning and Ryan working on his sixth no-hitter, veteran second baseman Willie Randolph lifted a high foul ball down the right field line.

Sierra, drifting toward the stands, tracked it under pressure and made the catch in foul territory. It wasn't a highlight-reel grab, but it was clean, confident, and complete. And with that, the game was over. Ryan had done it again.

The Final Outs That Defined the Moment

While the spotlight naturally fell on Ryan's numbers, these final outs were reminders that even the most dominant pitchers need their defense. Howe and Sierra weren't just finishing games; they were part of the story. Each brought his own style: Howe with quiet dependability, Sierra with youthful energy and flair. Both made sure the moment ended cleanly.

In a career defined by strikeouts, it was often the ball in play that found a glove that secured Ryan's place in history.

And in those rare, pressure-packed ninth innings, Art Howe and Ruben Sierra were exactly where they needed to be.

Alan Ashby: A Catcher's Legacy

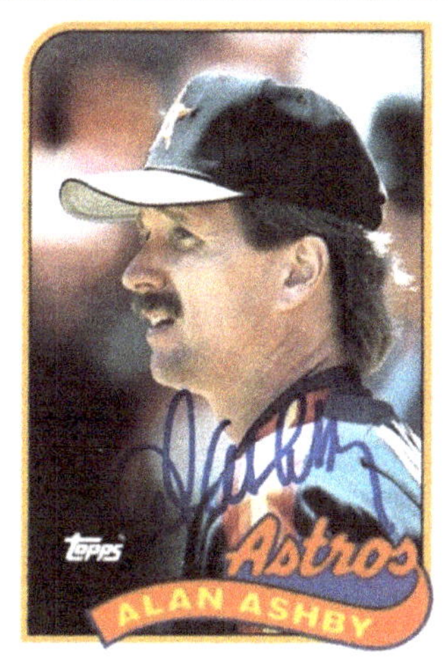

Every great pitcher leans on more than just their arm. For Nolan Ryan it often came down to trust, rhythm, and the steady hand behind the plate. During Ryan's years with the Houston Astros, that hand belonged to Alan Ashby.

Ashby wasn't flashy. He didn't chase headlines. But ask any pitcher who's stood alone on the mound, one mistake away from disaster, and they'll tell you the catcher is everything.

The strategy, the stability, the feel for when to press and when to settle it all runs through the man crouched behind home plate. For Ryan, few understood that role better than Ashby.

Their partnership spanned nearly a decade. By the time Ryan arrived in Houston, his reputation was well established: flamethrower, strikeout king, no-hitter machine. But even legends need someone to help channel the chaos. Ashby became that person, managing Ryan's arsenal with quiet precision, guiding him through moments that would further cement his legacy.

Two milestones stand out a reflection of both their careers woven together.

The first came in 1981, when Ryan threw his fifth career no-hitter, joining Sandy Koufax and Cy Young in the most exclusive of clubs. Ashby wasn't just catching pitches that night; he was orchestrating the game, balancing Ryan's overpowering fastball with pitch selection, tempo, and subtle reads of the Dodgers' lineup. Behind every zero on the scoreboard, there's a catcher calling pitches, adjusting defenses, and managing nerves. Ashby did it masterfully.

Four years later, it happened again. Ryan's 4,000th career strikeout was another unthinkable milestone that came with Ashby behind the plate. It wasn't just one pitch to Danny Heep; it was years of collaboration, countless innings of learning Ryan's tendencies, knowing how to draw the best out of him, especially as his career stretched into new territory.

But Ashby's ability to steady a pitching staff wasn't exclusive to Ryan.

Over the course of his Astros career, he became the only catcher in franchise history to guide three different pitchers through no-hitters — a testament to his instincts, preparation, and feel for the moment. In addition to Ryan's fifth no-hitter, Ashby caught Ken Forsch's no-hitter in 1979 and Mike Scott's in 1986, the latter clinching the division title for Houston. Few catchers have ever worn the mask for more no-hit history, and even fewer have done it with such calm consistency.

Some milestones belong to the pitcher the strikeouts, the no-hitters, the records but they're never achieved alone. Alan Ashby's fingerprints are all over Ryan's success in Houston.

His leadership behind the plate, his ability to manage one of the game's fiercest competitors, turned historic moments into shared triumphs.

Ashby never sought the spotlight. But in baseball's quiet spaces the bullpen meetings, the mound visits, the subtle nods between catcher and pitcher he was indispensable. For Nolan Ryan, there was no record without the partnership. For Alan Ashby, there was pride in the craft the responsibility of steadying a legend, pitch by pitch.

It's a reminder that in baseball, the catcher is far more than a target. He's a strategist, a calming presence, and at times, the only buffer between chaos and history. Alan Ashby filled that role with humility and precision, proving that every no-hitter and every milestone rests not just on an arm but on the bond of trust behind it.

Brad Arnsberg: Saving History

Brad Arnsberg's impact on Nolan Ryan's career might not be as widely recognized as some of Ryan's other milestones. Still, it played a crucial role in preserving one of the most historic achievements of all of Ryan's 300th career win.

The moment came on July 31, 1990, when Ryan, at age 43, faced the Milwaukee Brewers at Arlington Stadium. Ryan had pitched seven strong innings, allowing just one earned run, but it was Arnsberg, a 23-year-old reliever, who would be called upon to finish the game. Jeff Russell, the Rangers' regular closer, was out with an elbow injury, and Bobby Valentine was rotating through a short list of bullpen arms to close games. Arnsberg had thrown two innings just the day before and assumed another arm, perhaps Kenny Rogers, would get the call. But then the bullpen phone rang.

“I was pretty surprised,” Arnsberg later wrote. “Especially since I'd thrown two innings the day before. Next thing I knew, Valentine had gone to the mound, and as I was watching on the big screen directly above our bullpen, he was calling for the RHP?”

That right-hander was Arnsberg.

As he jogged in, his mother, watching from Medford, Oregon, dropped to her knees and prayed he wouldn’t blow it for Nolan. “Everything from leaving the bullpen mounds to getting the last four outs was kind of a blur,” Arnsberg admitted. “But I am sure thankful that my Mom’s prayer was answered!”

Arnsberg recorded the final four outs with steady command, preserving the 5–2 victory and etching his name into one of baseball’s most iconic box scores. “It’s kind of funny looking back,” he wrote. “Of the only five saves I ever recorded in the minor leagues and the big leagues, that was one of them!” [He actually finished with six total saves.]

But the connection between Arnsberg and Ryan didn’t end there. Years later, Arnsberg would coach Ryan’s son, Reid, in Charleston, South Carolina, as part of the Charleston RiverDogs organization. He had seen the Ryan legacy from both sides on the field, with the legend, and in the dugout, with the next generation.

Ryan's 300th win was more than another notch on a legendary resume. It was a testament to endurance, excellence, and the quiet threads of camaraderie that bind baseball teams together. Arnsberg may have been a young pitcher still carving out his role in the game, but for one night, in front of a roaring Texas crowd and a praying mother far away, he stood tall, helping a legend cross a final, monumental threshold.

"I'm very grateful to have had the opportunity," Arnsberg said, "not only to get the save in Nolan's 300th, but also to have gotten to play a couple of years around *the* legend himself."

Part 4: Power vs Power

The game's greatest hitters often found themselves on the wrong side of Ryan's fastball. These stories pit Ryan's fire against legendary bats, sometimes with explosive results.

Carl Yastrzemski: One Swing Shy of a No-No

Carl Yastrzemski was already a legend by the summer of 1972. In Boston, he had long since taken up Ted Williams' mantle in left field, and in the wider game, he stood as one of the few hitters who blended discipline, power, and endurance across decades. He was not a one-dimensional slugger, the type who chased fences and struck out freely. He was complete. Over twenty-three seasons, all with the Red Sox, Yastrzemski hit .285 with 3,419 hits, 452 home runs, and 1,844 RBIs and won seven Gold Gloves while appearing in 18 All-Star Games. He wasn't just the face of the Red Sox; he was the standard against which hitters of his generation were measured.

Two years before their defining encounter, Nolan Ryan had flirted with history for the first time. On April 18, 1970, pitching for the New York Mets, he took a no-hitter into the eighth inning against the Philadelphia Phillies before surrendering a single to Denny Doyle. Ryan struck out fifteen and walked six that day. It was a signature performance, wild and electric, and his first serious bid at a no-hitter.

But the batter who broke it up was a role player, a light-hitting second baseman who would finish his career with a .250 average and just two home runs.

For fans watching Ryan's career unfold, it felt like a pattern was beginning to emerge: close calls, dominant lines, but always one hit away. The no-hitter remained just out of reach.

On July 9, 1972, now with the California Angels, Ryan delivered one of the most dominant games of his young career. He struck out 16 Red Sox, including eight in a row, an American League record at the time, and fired an immaculate inning in the second: three strikeouts on nine pitches. The game was over in under two hours, a 3–0 win, and no Boston batter reached base after the first inning. It was Ryan at full throttle, still raw but learning how to channel it.

The only man to solve him that day was Yastrzemski.

Batting second in the top of the first, Yaz sent a clean single to right field. That was it, the only hit of the game. From that point forward, Ryan retired twenty-six consecutive batters. He carved through Boston's lineup with power and precision.

And yet, in a game defined by strikeouts, Yastrzemski never struck out.

He faced Ryan multiple times that night and never went down swinging or looking. He stood in, battled, and remained upright.

That detail matters.

Against Ryan across his career, Yastrzemski did what few could: he hit .333 in 45 plate appearances, a full 48 points higher than his already excellent career average. He struck out just six times in those matchups, an astonishing figure given Ryan's overpowering fastball and reputation for piling up strikeouts. For context, most left-handed hitters in the 1970s had little success against Ryan. Many avoided the box entirely if they had the choice. Yastrzemski not only faced him, but he also found ways to win.

That night in Anaheim wasn't just Ryan's second "almost" no-hitter. It was something rarer: a night when two greats shared the field, and each, in their own way, proved who they were. Ryan, with fire. Yastrzemski, with composure. And when everything else was silenced, when the bats went quiet and the dugouts emptied out pitch after pitch, it was

Yaz who stood alone with a hit on the board, and his name beside a moment Ryan couldn't erase.

CARL YASTRZEMSKI

MATCHUP SNAPSHOT

	PA	H	HR	BB	SO	AVG
vs. NOLAN RYAN	45	11	3	10	6	0.333
CAREER	13,991	3,419	452	1,845	1,393	0.285

Roger, Mark, and Barry: The Kings Who Couldn't Conquer Ryan

Only one man in baseball history faced Roger Maris, Mark McGwire, and Barry Bonds — the three single-season home run kings of the modern era. That man was Nolan Ryan, and true to form, he didn't just face them — he struck all of them out. Across their combined matchups, the trio went just 5-for-

28 against Ryan with zero home runs, a striking contrast to the power that would later define their legacies.

Each represented a generation of power. Maris held the single-season record for 37 years with 61 homers in 1961. McGwire shattered that with 70 in 1998.

Then came Bonds, who rewrote history with 73 in 2001. But before they became immortal for their home run records, they stepped into the batter's box against a legend whose heat and dominance transcended decades.

Roger Maris, the stoic Yankee with a compact swing, was already a two-time MVP and home run champ by the time he faced Ryan in the late 1960s. Maris finished his career with 275 home runs and a .260 average, but against Ryan, he was overmatched. In six plate appearances, he went 0-for-5 with two strikeouts and a walk, numbers that underscored how Ryan's fastball could overpower even one of the era's most decorated sluggers.

ROGER MARIS

MATCHUP SNAPSHOT

	PA	H	HR	BB	SO	AVG
vs. NOLAN RYAN	6	1	0	0	2	0.200
CAREER	5,846	1,325	275	652	733	0.260

Mark McGwire, known for his towering blasts and iconic home run chases of the 1990s, met Ryan near the end of Nolan's career. Big Mac slugged 583 home runs and hit .263 over his career. Against Ryan, he was 0-for-9 with one walk and struck out 6 times.

MARK MCGWIRE

MATCHUP SNAPSHOT

	PA	H	HR	BB	SO	AVG
vs. NOLAN RYAN	10	0	0	1	6	0.000
CAREER	7,660	1,626	583	1,317	1,596	0.263

Barry Bonds, the most feared hitter of his era and baseball's all-time home run leader with 762, also couldn't fully solve Ryan. Bonds was 4-for-14 in 15 plate appearances against him, a .286 batting average, and struck out 3 times.

It's easy to look at Ryan's numbers and marvel at the strikeouts and no-hitters. But moments like this, facing three of the greatest sluggers of all time, men who defined the power era, and getting the better of each one? That's legacy.

Ryan's longevity allowed him to span generations, but his dominance never faded. From Roger Maris in the fading light of baseball's early expansion years to Barry Bonds at the dawn of the modern power age, Nolan Ryan proved that no matter how many home runs you could hit, he could still make you miss

BARRY BONDS

MATCHUP SNAPSHOT

	PA	H	HR	BB	SO	AVG
vs. NOLAN RYAN	15	4	0	1	3	0.286
CAREER	12,606	2,935	762	2,558	1,539	0.298

Charlie Hustle: Rose vs Ryan

Baseball is built on legendary matchups, moments where the game's fiercest competitors meet head-on. Few were more captivating than the battles between Pete Rose, baseball's all-time hit king, and Nolan Ryan, the sport's most prolific strikeout artist. In 61 career showdowns, the unstoppable force of Ryan's fastball collided with Rose's relentless ability to put the ball in play.

They couldn't have been more different. Ryan embodied raw power, a blazing fastball, a devastating curve, and a record 5,714 strikeouts that left generations of hitters humbled.

Rose was a tireless grinder, a personified grit, with 4,256 career hits, the most in baseball history, fueled by hustle and uncanny hand-eye coordination.

Against Ryan, Rose fared better than most. He hit .261 (12-for-46) across their meetings, respectable when you consider how many of Ryan’s opponents walked away empty-handed. More telling, Ryan struck him out only nine times, a remarkable feat considering how few hitters escaped Ryan's grasp so often. Still, Rose never managed a home run off him. He scraped together singles, but Ryan kept him from inflicting lasting damage.

One of their most memorable encounters came in the 1981 All-Star Game. In the first inning, with the stage set for legends, Ryan struck Rose out, proving that even baseball’s toughest out could fall victim to Ryan’s overpowering arsenal.

Their rivalry was defined by mutual respect. Rose often named Ryan among the toughest pitchers he ever faced, acknowledging the challenge of solving his electric stuff. Ryan, for his part, respected Rose’s tenacity and relentless approach to the game. They were, in many ways, opposites but united by toughness, longevity, and a refusal to yield.

Ryan pitched an incredible 27 seasons, setting records unlikely to be touched. Rose played 24, his name etched atop the all-time hits list. Their careers were monuments to durability and competitive fire.

In the end, their clashes weren't about one player dominating the other. They were about two icons pushing each other to the edge, each forcing the other to earn every success. It wasn't easy. It wasn't one-sided. It was baseball at its purest: two legends, meeting at full strength, giving the game everything they had.

PETE ROSE

MATCHUP SNAPSHOT	PA	H	HR	BB	SO	AVG
vs. NOLAN RYAN	46	12	0	14	9	0.261
CAREER	15,861	4,256	160	1,566	1,143	0.303

The Hawk: Dawson Meets the Express

Few men in baseball's long history combined brute force and grace quite like Andre Dawson. "The Hawk" was a player of rare dimensions, an MVP, a slugger with over 400 home runs, and a perennial Gold Glove winner who patrolled the outfield with unrelenting precision. He played through pain, punished pitchers, and earned his place in Cooperstown through sheer will and transcendent ability.

Yet, for all the glory he accumulated, there remains one number that surprises: 25 strikeouts, more than any Hall of Famer ever suffered at the hands of Nolan Ryan.

That statistic carries weight not because Dawson was prone to failure, but because he rarely was.

He was, by any measure, one of the most complete hitters of his generation, and still, Ryan overpowered him more than any other in the Hall. It wasn't a sign of weakness. It was a testament to how often the two giants collided and how fiercely they competed.

“He was one of the more dominant power guys in the game,” Dawson reflected. “And for me, I always preferred those types of pitchers. It was strength against strength. It was a challenge for me to see how well I could do against a guy like that.”

Their first meeting occurred in May 1980, when a young Dawson emerged with the Montreal Expos, and Ryan was already feared as a strikeout king. Over 89 plate appearances, Dawson experienced the full range of emotions a hitter can feel when stepping into the box against raw electricity: tension, frustration, and at times, triumph.

“Nolan had that intimidating presence about him,” Dawson said. “A lot of guys didn't like to face him. I never felt intimidated by anyone; for me, it was about the challenge.

You knew he might get you, and you might have only marginal success at times. But you welcomed it, because of what it could potentially mean.”

One of Ryan's most significant career milestones came at Dawson's expense. On April 17, 1983, in the Astrodome,

Ryan blew a fastball past Dawson in the first inning, his 3,500th career strikeout. It placed Ryan in rarified air, joining only Walter Johnson and Gaylord Perry at the time. Dawson, like so many others, could only tip his cap.

But he was never just a victim in their exchanges.

On June 2, 1987, now with the Chicago Cubs, Dawson delivered one of the most devastating single-game performances of his career, and it came at Ryan's expense. In a 13–2 demolition at Wrigley Field, Dawson drove in seven runs. One of his hits, the one that still lingers in his memory, came just before a storm halted the game.

"He threw me a high fastball," Dawson recalled. "And for whatever reason, I swung. It was up around the chest, and I got on top of it and hit it out to left field. Just after that, there was this huge roar of thunder and lightning in the background. They stopped the game right then. I remember that one clearly."

Despite his power, Dawson often found himself chasing Ryan's high heat, a pitch that teased even the best. "Shawon Dunston used to ask me, 'Why are you swinging at that ball near your face?' And I'd tell him, 'It's just a matter of getting the barrel to it. I can see it. I may catch up to it, and chances are I may not, but I can see it.' And he'd laugh and say, 'Now I see why I make $300,000 and you make $3 million.'"

Still, Dawson made it clear: Ryan wasn't feared so much as respected, a rare combination of dominance and unpredictability. "When he had that breaking ball going, he was unhittable. And when you added that to a fastball, he might not have had full command of? That's when hitters got nervous. He had this persona: wild, overpowering, intense. You didn't hang too loose in the batter's box."

In total, Dawson managed four home runs, five doubles, and 13 RBIs against Ryan, a ledger that few can match. Their encounters were more than stat lines; they were tests of endurance, of pride, of mutual elevation. Ryan once said, *"Guys like Dawson made you work. You might get him today, but he'd make you pay tomorrow."*

To Dawson, the respect ran both ways. "He was historic. One of the most dominant pitchers ever. When he was on the mound, you saw the intensity in him. It was a joy, a pleasure, to be part of that."

Their duel was less a one-sided domination than a prolonged chess match, two legends meeting again and again in full force. The strikeout total tells one story, but the full account, and Dawson's own voice, tell another: of two titans trading blows, elevating one another, and forging a rivalry worthy of the game's highest halls.

ANDRE DAWSON

MATCHUP SNAPSHOT

	PA	H	HR	BB	SO	AVG
vs. NOLAN RYAN	89	20	4	4	25	0.244
CAREER	10,769	2,774	438	589	1,509	0.279

George Brett: A Nemesis for Nolan

When it came to facing Nolan Ryan, a pitcher known for blowing hitters away with heat and intimidation, very few batters could claim consistent success. But George Brett, the Kansas City Royals legend, stood in a league of his own.

Over the course of a 21-year Hall of Fame career, Brett collected 3,154 hits, batted .305, and won three batting titles. He wasn't just one of the best hitters of his generation; he was one of the best the game had ever seen. And when it came to Nolan Ryan, he did what almost no one else could: he held his ground.

In 115 plate appearances against The Ryan Express — more than most hitters ever got — Brett batted .287, with 29 hits and only 18 strikeouts. Even so, those 18 strikeouts were the most he ever accumulated against one pitcher. It wasn't dominance, but it was something arguably more impressive: consistency.

Among all players with at least 80 plate appearances against Ryan, Brett posted the highest career batting average, a rare distinction considering the devastation Ryan routinely dealt to even elite hitters.

With his smooth left-handed swing and uncanny ability to adjust to high velocity, Brett didn't try to overpower Ryan. He out-thought him. His approach was fearless and deliberate, rooted in bat-to-ball precision and remarkable timing, the very tools most hitters found ineffective against Ryan's blistering fastball and sharp-breaking curve.

Their matchups were less spectacle and more high art, two future Hall of Famers circling each other over decades, trading blows in a battle of wits and will. Brett forced Ryan to pitch differently, to lean on craft as much as power. Where others were overmatched, Brett remained steady, never intimidated, always prepared.

Over time, Brett's success became a quiet note in the larger score of Ryan's career, not a milestone moment, but a steady truth. Ryan may have struck out more batters than anyone in history, but George Brett was one of the few who consistently made him work for it.

In a game built on failure, Brett succeeded where most failed. Against one of the most overpowering arms the game has ever known, George Brett didn't flinch, and in doing so, he carved out his own space in the long shadow of The Express.

GEORGE BRETT

MATCHUP SNAPSHOT

	PA	H	HR	BB	SO	AVG
vs. NOLAN RYAN	115	29	0	14	18	0.287
CAREER	11,624	3,154	317	1,096	908	0.305

Will Clark: A Star's First Swing

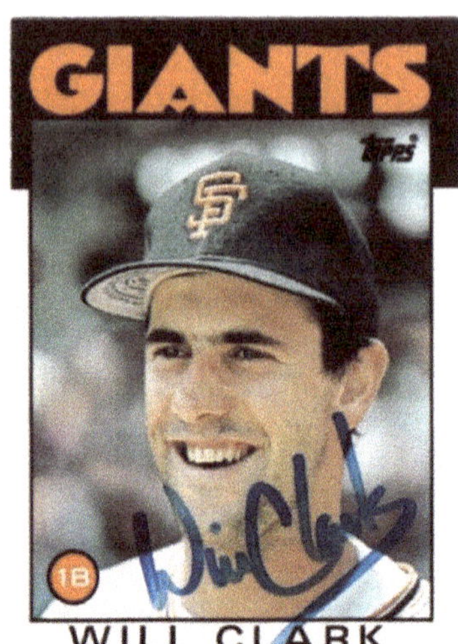

April 8, 1986, was a memorable day for both Nolan Ryan and a young slugger named Will Clark, who was making his major league debut for the San Francisco Giants. Clark, known for his smooth left-handed swing and impressive potential, would face the legendary Nolan Ryan in his very first at-bat, setting the stage for a dramatic encounter between one of the greatest pitchers of all time and a rising star in the game. This moment is a perfect illustration of how a player's first major league at-bat can become intertwined with the legacy of a legend because Clark's debut was anything but ordinary.

Before that day, Clark had already established himself as a highly touted prospect in the minors, where his early performances created a buzz throughout the baseball world. He made an immediate impact in professional baseball, famously homering in his first at-bat at every level — Class

A, Double-A and Triple-A — a feat that felt less like coincidence and more like a declaration that he belonged wherever the game placed him.

His minor league journey was marked by a meteoric rise, earning him quick promotions through the San Francisco Giants' system.

The stakes were far higher when he stepped into the box at the Astrodome, facing Nolan Ryan, still a dominant force, even in his 20th major league season. Ryan, known for his overpowering fastball and knee-buckling curve, presented a daunting challenge for any hitter, let alone a rookie. But Will Clark was no ordinary rookie.

Clark took Ryan's first pitch, a curveball, for a called strike. He then watched the second pitch, a fastball, miss outside the strike zone. With the count even at 1-1, Clark locked in. The third pitch came in, and Clark turned on it with authority, sending the ball soaring over the center field wall for a home run in his very first major league at-bat. The stunned Astrodome crowd watched as the 22-year-old circled the bases, his debut immortalized in a single swing. It wasn't just a hit; it was a thunderclap of a first impression, a message to the baseball world that Will Clark had arrived.

That home run became an iconic moment not just in Clark's career, but in Ryan's, too.

Clark would go on to become one of the most feared left-handed hitters of his era, with six All-Star appearances, a Gold Glove, and a Silver Slugger., But remarkably, his success against Ryan didn't stop with that first swing. Will Clark would go on to hit more home runs (six) off Nolan Ryan than any other player ever did, a stat that underscores the unique connection between the two players.

For Ryan, it was a testament to the never-ending challenge of facing the next generation of talent, even as his own legend continued to grow.

He struck out thousands and dominated lineups for decades, but some hitters, like Clark, found a way to solve the puzzle. That debut shot was just the beginning of a rivalry that added depth to Ryan's story and further elevated Clark's.

Their careers would follow different trajectories. Ryan pitched until age 46, while Clark eventually retired at 36, but that moment in Houston forever linked them. One was the face of baseball's past and present; the other, a glimpse of its future. And it all started with a 1-1 fastball that never came back.

Part 5: Fights, Ejections & Flashpoints

Ryan wasn't just a master of strikeouts; he was the center of unforgettable baseball drama. This part explores the confrontations and chaotic moments that tested Ryan's temper, toughness, and control.

Bo Jackson: A Bloody Show of Toughness

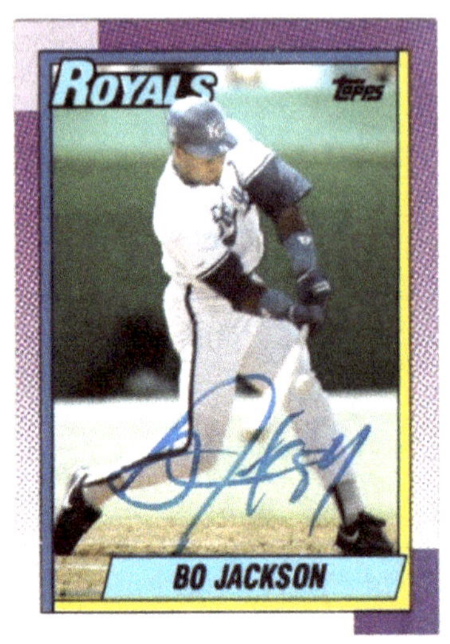

On September 8, 1990, Nolan Ryan took the mound for the Texas Rangers against the Kansas City Royals, still as fiery and fearless as ever at age 43. In the top of the second inning, the legend faced off against Bo Jackson, one of the most explosive athletes baseball had ever seen.

Jackson, known for his rare combination of speed and raw power, hit a scorching one-hopper back up the middle. The ball struck Ryan squarely in the face, splitting his upper lip and causing immediate bleeding. He reeled momentarily, blood streaming from his mouth, but he never left the game.

Without missing a beat, Ryan picked up the ball and, in a moment of near-unbelievable calm, threw Jackson out at first. Then, as if impervious to pain, he wiped the blood off his chin and kept pitching.

During the changeover between innings, Ryan received several stitches in the dugout to close the gash on his lip. But that was it. No exit. No dramatics. Just stitches, grit, and more fastballs.

He stayed in the game and went on to pitch seven full innings, allowing just three hits and striking out seven. The Rangers won 5–4, but the box score couldn't begin to capture what fans had witnessed: a 43-year-old warrior shaking off a shot to the face and carrying on as if nothing had happened.

That night didn't just showcase Bo Jackson's bat speed; it cemented Nolan Ryan's place in the pantheon of baseball's toughest competitors. The blood-streaked jersey became a lasting image, a symbol of Ryan's refusal to back down.

Rich Garcia: The Steady Hand Beneath the Chaos

1990 T&M Sports

In the high-pressure world of Major League Baseball, few figures commanded more quiet respect than umpire Rich Garcia. For nearly 25 years, Garcia was the steady hand behind home plate, a familiar presence on the foul lines, and, when needed, the authoritative voice that settled chaos. His career unfolded during one of baseball's most turbulent eras, the late 20th century, when the sport was shifting under the weight of larger contracts, evolving traditions, and the growing scrutiny of television audiences.

Garcia wasn't known for chasing headlines, but history had a way of finding him.

His résumé reads like a tour through some of baseball's most pivotal moments:

He was on the field for David Wells' perfect game in 1998, behind the scenes during the infamous Jeffrey Maier home run controversy in the 1996 ALCS, and at the heart of heated postseason battles from coast to coast.

However, two of Garcia's most unlikely intersections with history came courtesy of the same man, Nolan Ryan, the Texas fireballer whose legendary toughness spanned four decades. Garcia would become forever linked to Ryan, not through accolades or awards, but through a pair of unforgettable, rule-defining moments: handing Ryan the only ejection of his 27-year career, and later officiating the most famous mound charge in baseball history.

The Night Nolan Ryan Was Tossed

By August 6, 1992, Nolan Ryan was deep into the twilight of his career, still intimidating, still proud, but on this humid Texas evening, noticeably off his game. His pitches missed their spots. His frustration showed. And umpire Rich Garcia, working behind the plate, could feel the pressure building.

"He wasn't really having a good game," Garcia recalled. "In fact, I also ejected José Canseco earlier on. Things were already tense."

In the seventh inning, Royals speedster Willie Wilson fouled off a pitch with a sharp, aggressive swing. Ryan, never one to shy away from sending a message, approached the plate with a few choice words. Wilson didn't take kindly.

"Willie turned to me and said, 'Did you hear what he said?'" Garcia remembered.

"I told him, 'Yes, I did.' He asked, 'What are you going to do about it?' I said, 'I'm not going to do anything about it. What are you going to do about it?"

Wilson lashed a triple down the line, bringing the crowd to life and the tension to a boil. Ryan's scowl deepened. His competitive fire hadn't dimmed, but something else was about to ignite.

With runners on second and third in the eighth, Wilson came up again. Garcia noticed Rangers manager Toby Harrah heading to the mound. It looked like Ryan's night was done.

But Ryan waved him off.

"Nolan started shaking his head like, 'No, I ain't coming out. I got one more thing to do here," Garcia said. "I knew exactly what was going to happen."

The first pitch missed wide. The second hit Wilson's leg.

"There's no doubt in my mind it was intentional," Garcia said. "Everybody knew it was coming. Willie was yelling before the ball even hit him."

Garcia made the call: Nolan Ryan was ejected for the first and only time in his 27-season career.

“After the game, I found out that was the first time he’d ever been thrown out,” Garcia said. “Tossing a guy who never gets tossed is different; it’s like throwing the Pope out of the game.”

Ryan didn’t protest. Not really. “He tried to tell me he didn’t throw at him,” Garcia said, laughing.

“But with his southern drawl, he said, ‘If I really wanted to hit him, I would’ve hit him in the eye.’”

The fans in Arlington didn’t take it well. Seat cushions handed out as a promotional giveaway came raining down from the stands. The field turned into a mess. Garcia and his crew paused the game, sorted out the chaos, and eventually let the night come to an uneasy close.

It wasn’t the most famous ejection in baseball history. But for Garcia, it was unforgettable. A moment when authority met legacy, when the game’s unwritten rules collided with its very real ones.

And in the middle of it all stood Nolan Ryan, walking off the mound not in triumph, but in silence.

If ejecting Ryan was unexpected, Garcia's next brush with history was all but inevitable. Less than a year later, on August 4, 1993, Garcia was again the crew chief as the White Sox faced the Rangers in Arlington, a night that turned into one of the most replayed brawls in baseball history.

Rumors had been circulating before the first pitch.

"We heard there was tension," Garcia explained. "I don't know where the rumors started, but the White Sox were upset. Supposedly, they said if Ryan hit one of their guys, they were going to charge the mound."

Sure enough, early in the game, Robin Ventura, the 26-year-old White Sox star, took a fastball to the elbow. Ventura initially started toward first base, then veered left, sprinting toward the mound.

“He beat me there,” Garcia laughed. “I was close, but he made a beeline. And then, they started fighting.”

Ryan, nearly twice Ventura’s age at 46, showed no hesitation. He grabbed Ventura in a headlock and delivered a flurry of punches, a surreal, slow-motion collision of baseball generations.

As the chaos unfolded, Garcia stayed composed. Once the pile was cleared, the umpiring crew huddled.

“One of the guys asked, ‘What are we going to do with Ryan?’” Garcia said. “I told him, ‘We’re not doing anything with Ryan. We’re getting rid of Ventura.’”

Ejecting Ventura was automatic; charging the mound always was. But Garcia drew criticism for leaving Ryan in the game.

“I wasn’t going to throw him out,” Garcia stated firmly. “He defended himself. What’s he supposed to do? If you start tossing pitchers every time someone charges the mound, that’s not the right thing to do.”

White Sox manager Gene Lamont protested furiously. Garcia ejected him, too.

Afterward, players in the dugout continued chirping. Garcia called out one vocal pitcher: “You want a piece of Nolan? Get him. Otherwise, shut up.” The heckler disappeared down the runway.

Order restored, the game continued. The brawl, however, became baseball legend.

“I don’t hear too many people complain that Ryan stayed in the game,” Garcia said. “Everybody got a big kick out of the fact he was punching [Ventura] in the head. It happened the way it should have.”

The league agreed. Garcia filed his report, and no further action was taken.

For Rich Garcia, those two collisions with Nolan Ryan weren’t just isolated moments; they became unlikely markers in a long and respected umpiring career. In a profession often defined by routine, they stood out as rare instances where baseball’s larger-than-life mythology crossed paths with the everyday responsibility of enforcing the rules.

The ejection of Nolan Ryan remains one of the most improbable footnotes in the game’s history.

For Garcia, it underscored the idea that even legends aren't immune to accountability. It reinforced his role as an impartial figure in a sport where reputation often collides with responsibility. In that moment, he became the only umpire to send the Express off the field not by pitch count, but by rule of conduct.

The Ventura fight added a different layer to a flashpoint of baseball's old-school toughness clashing with the boldness of a younger generation. Garcia's decision to eject Ventura but let Ryan stay on the mound reflected a nuanced understanding of the game's unwritten codes. It was about context, intent, and fairness in an environment where those lines were often blurred.

Together, those events reflect Garcia's place in the fabric of baseball history. He wasn't just an umpire calling balls and strikes; he was a steady figure navigating the friction points between eras, personalities, and evolving expectations. His legacy is one of quiet authority, measured not by controversy. Still, there were rare and unforgettable moments when baseball's mythology brushed up against the rulebook, and he was there to make the call.

Morganna: A Double Play with Nolan Ryan

Morganna, known across ballparks as the "Kissing Bandit," never threw a pitch or swung a bat, yet carved out her own peculiar place in baseball history. Her fame came not from the diamond, but from sprinting onto the field, barreling in heels and low-cut tops to plant kisses on some of the game's biggest stars. What began in the late 1970s as a one-time stunt at a Cincinnati Reds game became a beloved running sideshow across major league ballparks.

Her list of conquests included legends like George Brett, Pete Rose, and Johnny Bench. But perhaps her most memorable caper came on May 1, 1988, in the Astrodome, when she charged the mound in the middle of a game to kiss Nolan Ryan, then 41 years old and still fanning hitters for the Houston Astros.

"Nolan Ryan is one of the greatest ball players of our time," Morganna later recalled in a handwritten letter. "He was so funny when I jumped the fence in Houston and ran out to kiss him. Nolan was on the mound. He dropped down on one knee. I told him the fans sent me to kiss him on the cheek, and I did."

What followed was a moment as spontaneous as it was endearing. Beside the mound stood shortstop Dickie Thon, newly returned from a brutal facial injury that had sidelined him for nearly a year. Morganna, never one to waste an opportunity, turned to Ryan and asked, "Should I go on over and give Dickie Thon a kiss to welcome him back?" Ryan grinned and replied, "You'd better hurry, the cops are right behind you!"

"That was my only double play in baseball," Morganna wrote, signing off simply: *Your Bosom Buddy, Morganna.*

The moment brought laughter to the Astrodome and showcased a lighter side of Ryan, whose usual demeanor on the mound was as serious as the heat he threw. He struck out nine that day. But for a brief moment, even baseball's fiercest competitor had to smile.

Part 6: Behind the Legend

Even a legend needs a support system. From the catchers who read every batter's weakness to the coaches and trainers who fine-tuned Ryan's mechanics, this section honors the unsung heroes who made Nolan Ryan's dominance possible. These stories reveal how sharp minds, steady hands, and strategic brilliance helped extend the career of one of baseball's fiercest competitors and how those working behind the scenes became just as crucial to the legend as the man on the mound.

Bobby Valentine: The Catch and the Command

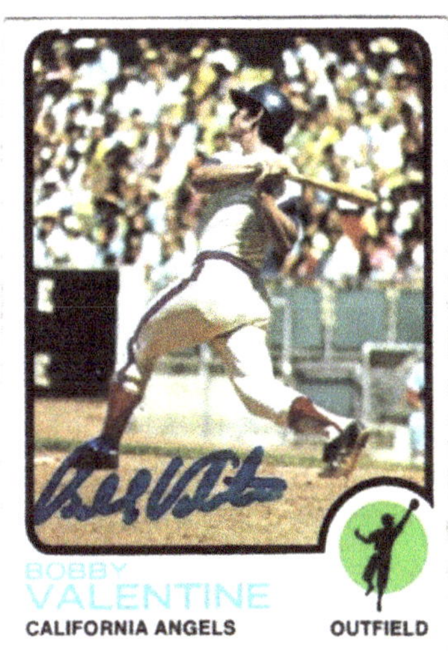

On May 15, 1973, the California Angels were locked in a battle with the Kansas City Royals, and on the mound, Nolan Ryan was on the verge of something special. His no-hitter was intact, but with each passing inning, the tension at Anaheim Stadium thickened. The Royals were starting to put better swings on the ball, and every defensive play took on heightened importance.

Then came the eighth inning, a moment that could have unraveled it all. With two outs, Royals catcher Ed Kirkpatrick sent a sinking line drive into center field, the kind of hit that so often ends a no-hit bid. Bobby Valentine, playing center field that night, broke in immediately. Known more for his grit and baseball instincts than raw speed, Valentine charged hard, dropped to his knees, and snared the ball just inches off the grass. It was a gutsy, all-out effort that preserved Ryan's no-hitter and drew a roar from the crowd.

Without Valentine's fearless read and split-second reaction, history might have taken a different path.

That catch wasn't just an out; it was the turning point that allowed Ryan to finish what he started. Moments later, as the ninth inning arrived, the no-hitter remained alive, thanks in no small part to the center fielder who made the play of the night.

But Valentine's connection to Ryan didn't end with their days in Anaheim. Years later, after both had moved on from their playing careers with the Angels, Valentine would cross paths with Ryan again, not as a teammate, but in a role that would once more shape Ryan's journey.

By the mid-1980s, Bobby Valentine had transitioned from player to manager, taking over the Texas Rangers in 1985 at just 35 years old, the youngest manager in the majors at the time. His tenure would prove formative for a franchise in search of an identity. And in 1989, when the Rangers signed Nolan Ryan, Valentine was presented with the rare challenge of managing a living legend still capable of greatness but now deep into his 40s.

Valentine understood that Ryan didn't need to be reinvented; he needed to be supported. While many managers might have shortened the leash on a pitcher his age, Valentine gave Ryan the autonomy to stick to the preparation routines that had carried him through two decades. Ryan had his own approach to conditioning, throwing, and recovery, which was far more rigorous than the norm. Valentine ensured that the coaching staff worked around those needs rather than against them.

Valentine also played a key role in handling Ryan's workload smartly.

He didn't hesitate to pull Ryan when there were signs of trouble, like in 1989, when he removed Ryan mid-game due to a minor hamstring strain, prioritizing longevity over short-term results. But when Ryan was rolling, Valentine let him run. That confidence paid off in historic fashion. Under Valentine's watch, Ryan threw two more record-breaking no-hitters: the sixth in 1990 against the Athletics, and the record-breaking seventh in 1991 against the Blue Jays, at age 44.

The manager-pitcher dynamic wasn't just about innings and pitch counts; it was about managing the aura of Nolan Ryan.

Valentine leveraged Ryan's presence in the clubhouse, understanding that the way Ryan prepared, competed, and held teammates accountable had a ripple effect. Younger pitchers, such as Kevin Brown and Kenny Rogers, watched Ryan work and absorbed those lessons, helping to build a new pitching culture in Texas.

Strategically, Valentine didn't shy from matching Ryan against elite lineups. He often kept Ryan slotted into high-leverage starts, series openers, marquee matchups, and games that drew attention. It was a bet not only on Ryan's ability to compete, but also on his draw as a box-office attraction. With Ryan on the mound and Valentine pulling the strings, the Rangers were no longer an afterthought.

Valentine's leadership helped extend Ryan's dominance into an age few pitchers ever reached, guiding him through injuries, milestone moments, and the daily grind with an instinctive understanding of when to push and when to protect.

It was a relationship built not on command, but on collaboration, two baseball minds who first crossed paths in the outfield of Anaheim, now navigating history from the dugout in Arlington.

From the diving catch that preserved Ryan's first no-hitter in 1973 to the carefully managed brilliance of his final ones in Texas, Bobby Valentine's fingerprints were quietly present at some of the most significant points in Nolan Ryan's journey. Not every influence in baseball is loud. Some, like Valentine's, are steady, smart, and essential.

Tom House: The Secret to Ryan's Longevity

Tom House, a former pitcher who became one of the pioneers of modern pitching mechanics and player development, had a profound influence on Nolan Ryan's career, particularly in the later stages of his Hall of Fame journey. House's impact wasn't simply in pitch sequencing or delivery tweaks it came from a scientific and holistic approach to training that helped Ryan defy the aging process and pitch at an elite level well into his 40s.

Before House became known as a pitching coach and biomechanical expert, he played for several teams in an 11-year Major League career (1967–1977), including the Braves, Red Sox, and Rangers. A left-handed reliever, House wasn't a superstar, but he was a student of the game.

His exposure to the mechanics of pitching and the toll it takes on a body laid the groundwork for what would become a revolutionary coaching career.

After retiring from the game, House devoted himself to the science of throwing.

In 1979, he founded the Rod Dedeaux Research and Baseball Institute at USC, where he began a deep study of biomechanics, examining how the body moves during a pitch and how to optimize that motion for performance and injury prevention. His approach included strength training, flexibility, nutrition, and recovery techniques, all of which were largely foreign concepts to baseball training at the time.

By the late 1980s, House's pioneering work was beginning to gain traction, and that's when his path intersected significantly with Nolan Ryan.

"Nolan signed a free agent contract with the Texas Rangers, where I was the major league pitching coach," House said. "I had known Nolan in the minor leagues, and I was a minor league pitching coach with the Astros when Nolan was there. The common denominator between us back then was Gene Coleman, the Astros' strength coach."

The Rangers' leadership at the time played a pivotal role in creating the conditions that drew Nolan Ryan to Texas. Both general manager Tom Grieve and manager Bobby Valentine had once been teammates of Ryan earlier in their playing careers, and now, in positions of influence, they were looking for innovative ways to improve player performance and longevity.

They weren't bound by convention and were receptive to science-backed approaches that prioritized biomechanics, strength training, recovery, and mental preparation. As House described it, "both were young free thinkers about ways to improve the health and performance of players on their roster."

It was this environment, forward-thinking leadership, and a willingness to embrace new methods that drew Ryan in. "Nolan actually signed with the Rangers for the science involved in biomechanics, functional strength, nutrition, and sleep for recovery and mental-emotional management," House explained. "Also, the Rangers allowed Nolan to have full access with family at home and on the road."

By 1989, Ryan was 42 years old. While still a force on the mound, signs of wear were beginning to emerge. House helped overhaul Ryan's training by focusing on recovery, mobility, and full-body conditioning rather than just arm strength. Ryan's routine now emphasized lower body and core strength, flexibility, and crucially, rest.

The House's philosophy was clear: keep the body functional, and the arm will follow. Ryan's velocity remained astonishing for his age. More importantly, he avoided the kinds of injuries that usually force pitchers into retirement.

Under House's guidance, Ryan pitched his sixth and seventh no-hitters at age 43 and 44 and notched his 5,000th strikeout, all while maintaining a fastball velocity that baffled hitters and defied the record books. Ryan credited his ability to pitch effectively into his mid-40s to House's training methods.

The results weren't just anecdotal; they helped usher in a new standard of training across Major League Baseball. What House implemented with Ryan became a prototype one adopted by other pitchers, coaches, and eventually organizations.

Biomechanics, recovery science, and mental preparation became foundational pillars in modern player development.

When Nolan Ryan retired in 1993 after 27 seasons, it was more than a farewell to a legend. It was proof of what was possible when traditional grit met modern science. And Tom House, once a journeyman lefty, had become one of the most influential pitching minds in the history of the game.

In House's words, Ryan's time with the Rangers wasn't just a final act it was "a commitment to innovation and longevity," built on trust, science, and a shared belief that greatness doesn't have to fade with age.

Part 7: Generations & Lineages

Baseball families often build legacies through bloodlines, fathers paving the way, sons chasing the greatness of their own. But few expected those legacies to collide with Nolan Ryan's fastball. This section follows the rare stories where two generations faced the same fate against Ryan, as baseball's most celebrated names, Griffey, Bonds, and Alomar learned that time may pass, but the heat stays the same.

Generational Strikeouts: Two Generations, One Result

Baseball, more than most sports, reveres its lineages. Fathers pass down gloves, swing mechanics, and whispered stories of greatness. Sons inherit the weight of the family name and the spotlight that comes with it. But there's one lineage few families hoped to share, that of being struck out by Nolan Ryan.

Over the course of his unprecedented 27 seasons on the mound, Ryan faced down not only the rising stars of each era but often their fathers before them.

His career stretched so long, spanned so many eras, that entire family legacies passed through his strike zone and often trudged back to the dugout after three futile swings.

The list reads like a baseball family tree rooted in both talent and longevity:

The Schofields — Dick Sr. & Dick Jr.

Dick Schofield Sr. broke into the big leagues in 1953, nearly a decade before Nolan Ryan made his MLB debut. Known for his sure glove and steady presence, Schofield carved out a 19-year career as a utility infielder, hitting .227 along the way. Their careers overlapped briefly, but the real generational mark came later, when Ryan faced Dick Schofield Jr., a defensive-minded shortstop in his own right.

Schofield Jr. spent 14 seasons in the majors, batting .230 over his career. Though not known for his offense, he shared something rare with his father both recorded strikeouts at the hands of Nolan Ryan, a symbol of how far Ryan's career stretched beyond the average timeline.

The Franconas — Tito & Terry

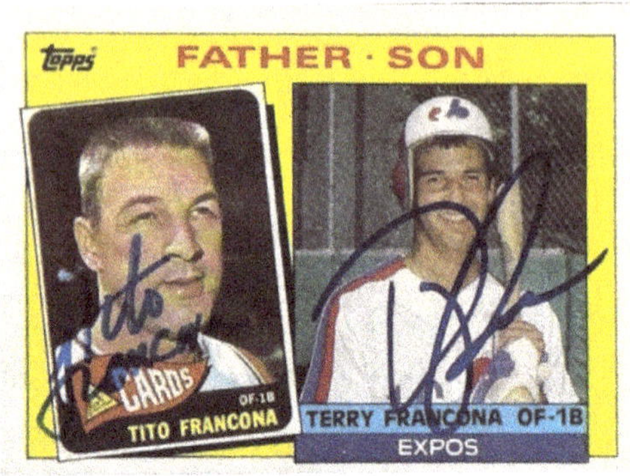

© 1985 The Topps Company, Inc.
All rights reserved
Francona autos courtesy of the Guina Collection

Tito Francona was a reliable outfielder and first baseman whose best years came in the 1960s. He finished his career with a solid .272 batting average and a reputation as a tough at-bat. By the time Tito stood in against Ryan, the veteran was in his twilight, while Ryan was just beginning to cement his place as a strikeout artist.

Years later, Tito's son Terry, who'd go on to become a respected manager with World Series titles to his name, stepped into the box against Ryan as a young player. Terry hit .274 over his brief major league career, and like his father, couldn't escape Ryan's legacy.

Their connection to Ryan weaves through both the batter's box and the dugout, where Terry would one day manage pitchers who tried but rarely succeeded to emulate Ryan's dominance.

The Wills — Maury & Bump

Few players electrified the game the way Maury Wills did. The 1962 MVP, Wills revolutionized base stealing, swiping an astonishing 104 bags that year alone. He finished his career as a .281 hitter, but his speed meant staying off the bases was crucial for opposing pitchers, something Ryan handled by keeping hitters guessing.

Maury's son, Bump Wills, followed the family tradition of speed and versatility, batting .273 over six seasons. Like his father, Bump couldn't outrun the inevitable; both Wills' men fell victim to Ryan's fastball, a reminder that no amount of wheels or baseball heritage could entirely escape his grasp.

The McRaes — Hal & Brian

Hal McRae was pure intensity at the plate, aggressive, fiery, and never backing down from a challenge. His .290 career batting average reflected his consistency and toughness, but facing Ryan was a different battle.

The two collided in countless contests, Ryan often having the upper hand, using a biting curveball and overpowering fastball to neutralize Hal's competitive edge.

Brian McRae, more measured but still a capable big leaguer, carried the family name into the '90s, posting a .261 career average.

When he faced Ryan late in Nolan's career, the result mirrored his father's, another chapter in a family story intertwined with strikeouts and one of baseball's most feared arms.

The Griffeys — Ken Sr. & Ken Jr.

Ken Griffey Sr. was a cornerstone of Cincinnati's Big Red Machine, a .296 lifetime hitter who played with swagger and efficiency. He faced Ryan at the height of National League showdowns, often as part of those intense, postseason-caliber battles where every pitch mattered.

But it's his son, Ken Griffey Jr., who became baseball royalty, "The Kid," destined for the Hall of Fame. Griffey Jr. finished his illustrious career with a .284 batting average, 630 home runs, and countless highlights. Yet even he couldn't entirely solve Ryan's puzzle:

Against Nolan, Junior hit .240, 6-for-25, though he did manage to tag Ryan for two home runs and eight RBIs. Despite flashes of brilliance, Ryan still carved out strikeouts, proving that even prodigies weren't immune to the sharp sting of experience.

It was one of baseball's most poignant images: a young Griffey Jr., brimming with promise, facing a grizzled Ryan whose legacy was already secure.

The Bonds — Bobby & Barry

Bobby Bonds electrified the game with his rare combination of power and speed.

One of the original 30–30 threats, Bonds stacked five seasons with at least 30 home runs and 30 stolen bases, reshaping expectations for what a leadoff hitter could be. His career .268 batting average reflected his overall consistency, but Nolan Ryan was a different challenge entirely.

In their head-to-head matchups, Ryan silenced Bonds to the tune of a .143 batting average, just 2-for-14, with five strikeouts. Even a player as dynamic as Bobby, who could disrupt games with a single swing or stolen base, found little room to breathe against Ryan's fastball.

Barry Bonds, of course, took the family legacy and rewrote the record books entirely. Seven MVP awards, 762 home runs, and a .298 career average made him one of the most feared hitters the game has ever seen. But in his 15 plate appearances against Ryan, Barry hit .286, managing four hits, but never sending one over the fence.

Two generations of Bonds. Legendary careers. Yet both left humbled by the same opponent, Ryan's relentless precision and power.

Why These Numbers Matter

For most players, a 15-year career feels like a lifetime. Nolan Ryan's career outlasted not just eras, but entire bloodlines of baseball. Fathers who squared off against him in the 1970s watched from the stands as their sons faced the same fate a decade or two later. Some were future Hall of Famers.

Some were destined to manage World Series winners. Some, like the Griffey or Bonds, carried the weight of generational greatness on their shoulders.

It made no difference to Ryan.

The stat lines tell the story of batting titles, stolen bases, and home run records, yet time after time, these legacies intersected with the same barrier: Nolan Ryan on the mound. Whether it was the promise of youth or the hard-earned wisdom of veteran hitters, Ryan's fastball and curveball were the great equalizers across generations. This wasn't just a pitcher outlasting his peers; it was a career so impossibly long and dominant that it carved through baseball family trees like few others ever have.

And no family represents that more personally than the Alomar's.

Alomar: A Name Spanning Generations, Written in the Records

In the early 1970s, the California Angels clubhouse was a patchwork of baseball's rising talents and seasoned veterans, all converging in the sun-drenched, high-expectation swirl of Major League promise. Among them, a wiry, hard-throwing Texan named Nolan Ryan, freshly arrived from the New York Mets, was still refining his electric fastball into the force of nature it would soon become. Across the diamond stood Sandy Alomar Sr., a dependable infielder and consummate baseball man, known less for towering statistics and more for the quiet, steady reliability that earns the respect of every dugout. A native of Puerto Rico, Alomar had carved out a 15-year major league career with the Braves, Mets, White Sox, Angels, and Yankees. He was admired for his defense, versatility, and baseball IQ, the kind of player managers trusted to stabilize the infield and mentor younger teammates.

They were teammates in Anaheim, bound by the day-to-day rhythm of the game, batting practice, infield drills, clubhouse chatter, but also by something far more enduring: family. During those Angels years, a young Nolan Ryan, already gaining notoriety for the velocity of his fastball, took a moment to show Sandy's four-year-old son, Roberto, how to grip a baseball and throw it properly. No one in the clubhouse thought much of it, then, just a teammate sharing a moment with a friend's child. But in hindsight, it was the faint first chapter of one of baseball's most elegant generational arcs. That little boy, Roberto Alomar, would grow up to become one of the greatest second basemen the game has ever known: a 12-time All-Star, 10-time Gold Glove winner, two-time World Series champion, and eventual Hall of Famer. Over a 17-year career, he compiled 2,724 hits, 210 home runs, and 474 stolen bases, cementing his place among the most complete middle infielders of his generation.

But before Roberto's legacy took root, Nolan Ryan and Sandy Alomar Sr. would cross paths again, this time as opponents.

By 1974, Alomar Sr. had been traded to the New York Yankees, and Ryan, now the undisputed ace of the Angels, was piling up strikeouts at a historic pace. On August 25 of that year, under the late-summer sun, Ryan did what he had done to so many: he sent a fastball past a helpless bat and etched another milestone into the record books. Strikeout number 1,500 — and the batter? Sandy Alomar Sr.

It was a fitting milestone, but far from a routine strikeout. Alomar Sr. was no easy out, known for his contact skills, discipline, and toughness at the plate. Though he finished with a career batting average of .245, he was one of the few players who seemed to match up well against Ryan. In just 12 career at-bats against the future strikeout king, Alomar batted .333, a small but telling stat line that reflected his ability to battle against even the most overwhelming arms of the era. The 1,500th strikeout, then, wasn't just a number; it came against a respected veteran who had seen Ryan's best and never backed down.

But baseball, in its poetic, generational sprawl, wasn't finished with the Alomar family or Nolan Ryan.

Years later, Ryan found himself toeing the mound against the next wave of Alomar talent, Sandy Alomar Jr., a two-time All-Star catcher known for his strong arm and leadership behind the plate, and Roberto, the same child he once showed how to throw a baseball. The circle closed tightly on May 1, 1991, when Roberto Alomar, now a rising star with the Toronto Blue Jays, stepped into the batter's box with history hanging in the air. On that day, Nolan Ryan, now a grizzled 44-year-old veteran pitching for the Texas Rangers, was crafting one final masterpiece: his record-setting seventh no-hitter.

It ended with Roberto at the plate.

One more time, a Ryan fastball blurred past an Alomar. One more time, the game wrote its quiet, poetic echoes across generations. Roberto struck out swinging, securing the no-hitter and reaffirming that for all the years, teams, and legends that had come and gone, Nolan Ryan's fastball still had the final word.

In the end, Ryan didn't just pitch against Sandy Alomar Sr., he pitched against two of his sons, striking out all three in moments that stitched their family story forever into his own legend. Across decades, through generations, the Alomar name and the Ryan legacy remain interwoven, a reminder that in baseball, the most powerful connections often go deeper than box scores or record books can ever show.

Part 8: Cardboard Connections

Baseball cards don't just record careers, they preserve memories. This section shifts the focus from the field to the fans, exploring how Nolan Ryan's legend lived not only through strikeouts and no-hitters but in the hands of kids, the corners of shoeboxes, and the faded edges of cardboard. Here, we remember the myth as it was shaped by those who never faced his fastball but felt like they knew him anyway.

The Game You Could Hold

Before they were slabbed in plastic and sold at auction, baseball cards lived where kids did, in shoeboxes, jean pockets, and sunlit bedrooms thick with imagination. They weren't measured in grades or gloss, but in moments: the crackle of a wax pack, the chalky taste of gum, the thrill of pulling a name you knew from last night's radio broadcast.

Somewhere in those stacks waited Nolan Ryan — a young pitcher from Alvin, Texas, sharing his first Topps rectangle with a quiet left-hander named Jerry Koosman. He was half of a card, half of a story. For many kids, that small piece of cardboard was the first time they saw Ryan, not on a color TV or in the sports section, but in their own hands. It was the game you could hold.

Back then, a card wasn't a commodity.

It was a connection.

For kids who grew up with Ryan's rookie tucked between commons and gum wrappers, the stories didn't stop when the packs were opened; they only expanded.

Different Streets, Same Summer

Bob Clouston remembers it starting with his older brothers. Packs of '68s and '69s scattered across the floor, brothers dealing doubles, the quiet thrill of seeing your favorite face emerge from the stack. "Nearly every house on our street had kids," Bob said, "and there were countless trading sessions with our cards spread out on bedroom floors so we could wheel and deal."

By 1970, the collection felt like his. The players were his, too: Ernie Banks smiling in a batting stance, Rod Carew mid-throw, Don Kessinger's bat nearly pointing at the camera. Cubs and Twins and whoever else came in that day's pack became part of the rotating cast in Bob's homemade world.

Meanwhile, across another town, Steve Krick was doing the same, buying packs from the corner store, sitting on the curb with his friends, chewing five sticks of gum at once, and building a lineup out of dreams. "If I had 50 cents," Steve said, "I thought I was rich. I could buy 10 packs of cards, 50 cards! That was everything."

For both of them, cards weren't just things to have. There were things to do. You sorted them. Studied them. Played with them.

You turned them into teams and seasons and arguments over who was better. They weren't collectibles. They were companions.

Stats on the Back, Magic in the Hands

The back of the card was just as important as the front, sometimes more. Bob and his brother pored over numbers the way other kids memorized comic book lore. "The games were a reason to pore over the cards front and back," he said. "Probably more so the back than the front."

There were patterns to discover, legends to track. Hank Aaron's unshakable string of 30- and 40-homer seasons. Norm Cash's outlier year. The thrill of seeing a number you recognized and knowing it meant something.

Steve's favorite card, the 1967 Willie Mays, is creased now, a little wrinkled at the corners from years of handling. But that card was never meant to be pristine. It was meant to be held. "I would just study his stats," Steve said, "and hoped that one day I could be like him."

And somewhere in those same shoeboxes, kids flipped over the Ryan–Koosman rookie and read the fine print, minor league towns like Greenville and Jacksonville, earned runs and innings pitched that hinted at something just beginning. The numbers were ordinary: wins, losses, strikeouts, and walks. But to anyone looking closely, they whispered of something unformed yet inevitable, a fastball not yet famous, but already stirring beneath the surface.

To a kid, that was enough. A name. A pose. A stat line. The connection didn't need a PSA label; it needed heart.

They Weren't Perfect, They Were Yours

In those days, cards weren't protected; they were lived in. Carried around. Left in the sun. Bent from too many flips on the sidewalk. Some got defaced, or cut, or scribbled on, not out of disrespect, but out of use.

Bob remembered putting an X through Reds pitcher Ron Tompkins just to make sure everyone knew it was Johnny Bench in the lineup. Steve admitted to cutting rookie cards in half just to double his roster.

"The Ryan rookie is the most famous I cut in half," he said with a laugh. "But I had others too."

They weren't trying to destroy value. They were trying to *play the game.* And in doing so, they created a different kind of value one that couldn't be graded or sold.

A card with rounded corners wasn't ruined. It was rich with memory. Because that scuff on the edge? That was the time you won three flips in a row. That wrinkle? That was the pack of gum you shoved in your pocket with it.

Those weren't flaws. Those were footnotes.

And in the case of Nolan Ryan, every crease in those early cards carried a trace of childhood discovery a record of when he wasn't yet *The Ryan Express,* but simply another arm, another name, another reason to dream.

The Innocence of the Era

Before fantasy leagues. Before Beckett. Before eBay. There was a quiet kind of joy in collecting not to invest, but to belong. You weren't curating a portfolio. You were building a team. You were filling out a lineup card, mimicking Joe Morgan's stance in your backyard, holding a card up to the sky, and imagining what it would feel like to stand in that uniform.

The cards let you do that. They let you touch the game even if just for a moment.

Years later, as the hobby grew and the world of mint grades and auction blocks took hold, that same Nolan Ryan rookie card became the symbol of what was lost and what endured. Once traded on curbsides for spare doubles, now encased in acrylic and worth a fortune, it carried both the fingerprints of children and the weight of history.

To those who once owned it, it was never about the price. It was about the memory the feeling that, for a moment, you held the game itself in your hands.

When Cardboard Played Ball

Before the cards were tucked away in binders or sealed behind acrylic glass, they were drafted, flipped, shuffled, and sent charging around the bases on living room carpets and backyard dirt. For a generation of kids, baseball cards weren't the end of the game.

They were the beginning.

Because once you had the cards, the next step was obvious: you played.

Every Room a Stadium

Some kids built fields out of pillow baselines and Lego fences. Some turned a ruler and a crumpled paper wad into a bat and ball. Others just lined up teams on the floor, imagined the matchups, and let the stats on the back tell the story.

Bob Clouston remembers it clearly. "My brother remembers spreading them out on the floor of our tile basement bedroom and playing with a pencil and a marble. I remember using a ruler and a small wad of paper, a spitwad without the spit, because we did have a little respect for the cards."

These games were loose, barely structured. The idea was simple: hit the paper "ball" with the ruler and see where it landed. If it passed second base, maybe it was a double. If it rolled into the outfield of cards, it could be a home run. Each kid made their own rules, usually adjusted by the size of the room, the layout of the "field," and the imagination of the day.

Bob recalled organizing teams by city or color. "Cubs and White Sox were grouped together," he said, "perhaps as much for both teams having an orange circle in the '68 cards as them being Chicago teams." They didn't always play head-to-head. Often, it was solo play, just a kid and his league, managing both sides and announcing the plays softly to himself.

This wasn't collecting. This was baseball, reimagined.

Flips, Trades, and Sidewalk Legends

Card flipping was part luck, part skill, and all heart. You crouched near the wall or chalked-off line, holding your best card between your fingers like a poker chip. The goal? Flip it just right, end over end, corner over corner, so it landed closer to the target than anyone else's. Or landed face-up to match the pile. Or won in a round of "topsies," "leaners," or whatever local variation your friends swore was the real rule.

The prize was simple: you won the cards you beat.

Sometimes it was a friendly match. Other times, it was cutthroat. Stack against stack. Closest to the wall takes all. A single round could clean out your afternoon's collection or net you a new hero.

The cards didn't last long in these battles. Their corners softened. Their edges bruised. Asphalt left tiny scuffs that no amount of straightening could undo. But none of that mattered.

Because in those few airborne seconds, that piece of cardboard wasn't just a card. It was a risk. A reward. A heartbeat.

And when it landed right when it won, you got the best card on the playground; it was everything.

These were the games where legends were born, not in box scores or broadcast replays, but in the flick of a wrist, the bounce off the pavement, and the sound of one more card hitting the ground.

The Dice Rolled On

As Bob got older, the games got smarter. More structured. First came invented dice games, with six-sided charts and 36 potential outcomes. "We think we made up some kind of dice game with 36 different possibilities," he said. "Again, the setup was the fun part."

They'd assign outcomes strikeout, groundout, single, walk to each number combination (like 2-1, 2-2, etc.), then roll dice and use real player cards as lineups. Games usually ended quickly. Leagues rarely made it past a few games. But that wasn't the point.

Then came the game that stuck: Strat-O-Matic.

They got it in 1971, based on the 1970 season. "We did a full replay using the actual schedule," Bob said. "The Yankees beat the Cubs in the World Series. Both finished 2nd in their division in real life, so it wasn't that far-fetched."

Strat was serious. Every player had a custom card built from real-life stats. You rolled three dice, read the result from columns on the player's card, and tracked the outcome in notebooks or grease pencil boards. The stats were real. The matchups mattered.

"Danny Cater (.301 that year in real life) was the star of the Yankees," Bob remembered, "while Fergie Jenkins won 30 games in our replay for the Cubs. Marty Pattin, a decent pitcher for the hapless Brewers, spun the only no-hit game in our replay, IIRC."

Strat turned cards into seasons. It gave every decision weight. For Bob and for thousands of kids like him, it made you feel like a manager.

The Leagues We Built

Even before Strat-O-Matic, Bob and his brother were building custom leagues with nothing more than baseball cards and math. "We'd pick a starting lineup, add up the stats on the back AB, R, H, TB, RBI, and calculate team rankings," he said. "Whoever had the lowest total score across categories was the best team."

They'd assign rankings like a cross-country meet: #1 in batting average earned 1 point, #12 earned 12. Add them up. Lowest total wins.

And the standings changed all the time. A new card could tip the balance. "Every time I bought new packs of cards," Bob said, "I'd see which lineups got updated, then I'd recalculate their scores."

There were World Series matchups. The Reds beat the Orioles. Big stats like Tony Perez's .317 average and 40 homers could vault a team overnight. There was no dice, no ruler, just math and imagination.

Steve's version looked different, but the spirit was the same. He and his cousin used wiffle ball to bring players to life. "We'd choose teams or players from the Majors and make our lineups out," he said. "If you hit the ball into the alley on a fly, that was a single. If you hit it across the alley into the neighbor's yard, that was a double. Up against their garage wall, that was a triple. Into their driveway, a home run. And onto their garage roof that was a grand slam."

The neighbor ladies didn't appreciate it. "We lost a lot of balls that way," Steve said. "So that meant a trip down to the Western Auto store to buy another."

But the game never stopped.

Because the game wasn't on TV.

It was in the backyard.

The Cardboard Universe

Looking back, it's clear these weren't just games.

They were training grounds. For imagination. For math. For memory. For the beginnings of love for the sport, for the players, for the act of creating a world from a pile of paper and stats.

And for Bob, it was also something deeper. “I think collecting, trading, and playing with the cards stoked my interest in baseball much more than if I'd have treated them as collectibles.”

The rules weren't perfect. The cards weren't pristine. But the games?

The games were yours.

Because for one perfect stretch of summer, you weren't watching baseball.

You were playing it.

A Tale of Two Halves

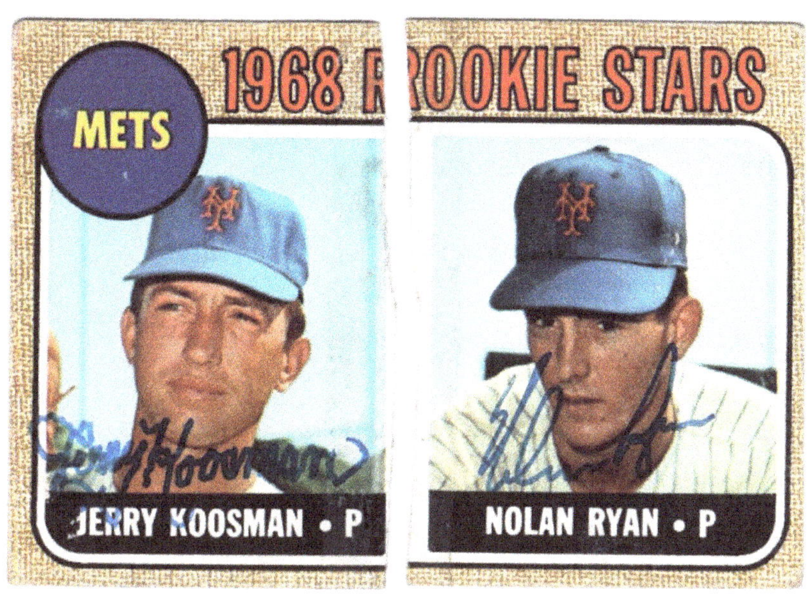

Somewhere in the early 1970s, maybe in a cluttered bedroom, maybe in a sunlit backyard, a kid made a decision that seemed ordinary at the time. He took a 1968 Topps rookie card, one that featured Jerry Koosman and Nolan Ryan, and cut it in half.

Why? No one knows. Maybe Koosman was his favorite. Maybe he just wanted each player on his own team. Or maybe, like so many kids back then, he saw the card not as a treasure but as a tool. Something to use. Something to play with.

Cards weren't sacred then. They were *accessible*. Folded into pockets, fanned across bedroom floors, or stacked for sidewalk flips. This card was no different. Its fate wasn't sealed in plastic, it was shaped by imagination, loyalty and maybe a pair of dull scissors.

But what's truly remarkable isn't just that it was cut.

It's that the two halves stayed together.

Across decades and who-knows-how-many trades, through sales, rediscoveries, or sheer luck, the pieces remained a pair separated, but never truly apart. Eventually, they found their way into my collection: imperfect, uneven, and completely unforgettable.

I didn't try to restore it. I didn't try to replace it.

Instead, I decided to honor its journey.

In July 2025, I sent each half on a path of its own again, but this time, not for play. Koosman's half went directly to him. Ryan's half went to the Nolan Ryan Foundation. Two envelopes. Two names. One story.

And then, almost poetically, they returned each on their own timetable, just as their careers had once unfolded.

Koosman, the early star, came first. His signature arrived on July 25, with the same reliability that had once defined his role in the Mets' rotation. Ryan, the flame-throwing phenomenon whose career would stretch longer and soar higher, followed two months later. His signature came back on September 25.

Now, they sit side by side again. Weathered. Split. Signed.

Whole, in a way they never were before.

They aren't pristine. Their corners are soft, their edges worn. But there's a gravity to them now, a weight that has nothing to do with dollars or condition. These halves tell a story that no mint-graded slab ever could.

Because this card lived, it was played with. Handled. Cut. Saved.

It passed through the hands of a kid who couldn't have known that one of these names would one day become legend. He didn't see an investment. He saw *players*. Koosman, the dependable ace. Ryan, the wild flamethrower who walked too many but threw harder than anyone.

That kid didn't ruin the card.

He gave it meaning.

And decades later, the signatures don't erase the damage; they *redeem* it. They remind us what cards have always been: bridges. Between teammates. Between decades. Between players and the kids who followed them.

Some cards are prized for their rarity.

This one is prized for its story.

It's not whole. But it is complete. Like Ryan's career itself, it endured creases, tests, and lasted far longer than anyone could've imagined — carrying Nolan Ryan forward, not as a headline, but as a constant.

Part 9: Legacy & Farewell

Ryan's influence didn't end when he left the mound. This final part reflects on how his career inspired others, how he was immortalized in baseball history, and the passing of the torch to future generations.

Randy Johnson: Passing the Torch

Nolan Ryan's career didn't end when he left the mound. For many fans, it had already been living elsewhere for years — in stories retold, moments replayed, and objects kept close long after the box scores were forgotten. By the time Nolan Ryan threw his final pitch in 1993, his name was already etched into baseball's history books. Seven no-hitters, 5,714 strikeouts, and an awe-inspiring 27 seasons in the majors — numbers that seemed untouchable. But Ryan's impact on the game extended far beyond the statistics. His influence would carry on, shaping the next generation of power pitchers who idolized him, studied him, and in some cases, received direct guidance from him. Among them was a young, lanky left-hander who would one day carve out a Hall of Fame career of his own: Randy Johnson.

In the early 1990s, Johnson had all the raw talent in the world. He stood an imposing 6-foot-10 and could touch 100 mph with his fastball, but he struggled mightily with control. His erratic delivery led to high walk totals, and many wondered if he'd ever harness his full potential. That's when fate, along with a little help from Nolan Ryan, intervened.

In 1992, Johnson sought out Ryan for advice, knowing that the veteran had once battled similar control issues early in his career. Ryan, who had tamed his own wildness to become a dominant force, gave Johnson a simple but powerful piece of advice: "Keep your head still." It was a small adjustment, but it made a world of difference. Johnson incorporated Ryan's suggestion, and his walk rate began to drop while his strikeout numbers continued to rise. The transformation was underway.

Johnson's dominance in the years that followed mirrored many aspects of Ryan's legendary career. Like Ryan, he became a strikeout machine, eventually amassing 4,875 K's, second only to Ryan himself. He also learned the value of conditioning and longevity, throwing a perfect game at age 40 and remaining an elite pitcher deep into his career, just as Ryan had done.

But Johnson wasn't the only pitcher Ryan influenced. Roger Clemens, another fireballer, shared a similar relentless work ethic, often crediting Ryan's legendary training regimen as a model for his own. Even Justin Verlander, who grew up watching Ryan pitch, later embraced Ryan's philosophy of throwing deep into games and maintaining velocity late into his career.

Ryan's influence extended beyond direct interactions; it was embedded in the way future pitchers approached the game. His belief in pitching aggressively, his commitment to fitness, and his refusal to accept limitations all became hallmarks of the power pitchers who followed. Every time a modern pitcher defies age, throws 100 mph in the late innings, or dominates a game with pure power, a piece of Ryan's legacy lives on.

While Nolan Ryan's name will forever be linked to his records, his greatest contribution to baseball may not be found in a stat sheet. It's in the pitchers he inspired, the careers he shaped, and the unmistakable impact he left on the game long after he threw his final pitch. In that way, Ryan's influence will never fade it will simply be passed down, generation to generation, like a well-placed fastball on the outside corner.

A Legend Immortalized

As Nolan Ryan walked away from baseball in 1993, the conversation wasn't about *if* he'd be enshrined in Cooperstown; it was *when*. The years following his retirement were filled with admiration and reflection, as the baseball world began to absorb the scale of his accomplishments fully. Writers, broadcasters, and fans all recognized the truth: Ryan hadn't just compiled a remarkable career; he had redefined the boundaries of what a pitcher could be.

By the late 1990s, Ryan's name was routinely spoken in reverent tones, often in the same breath as legends like Koufax, Gibson, and Seaver. His records were jaw-dropping: 5,714 strikeouts, a mark no one had come close to touching; seven no-hitters, a record that many believe will never be approached again; and a career that had spanned four decades and 27 seasons, an almost mythical feat of endurance and competitiveness.

As the 1999 Hall of Fame ballot approached, there was no mystery about his candidacy only how high the voting percentage would be. When the results were announced, Ryan received 491 of 497 possible votes, a staggering

98.79%, one of the highest totals in Hall of Fame history. He was inducted alongside fellow baseball greats George Brett and Robin Yount, forming one of the most iconic classes the Hall had ever seen.

The lead-up to induction day was filled with celebrations across all four cities that had been touched by Ryan's career: New York, Anaheim, Houston, and Arlington. Each team honored him in their own way, with commemorative nights, video tributes, and a flood of fan appreciation. Ryan himself chose to enter the Hall of Fame as a Texas Ranger, the team where he had spent the final, unforgettable chapter of his playing days and where his legend had reached its most mythic form.

On July 25, 1999, Ryan stood on the podium in Cooperstown, dressed in a crisp suit and Hall of Fame cap, delivering a speech that was equal parts humble and heartfelt. He spoke about the people who shaped his life: his wife, Ruth, his family, his coaches, and the scouts who first saw potential in a lanky Texas teenager. He thanked his teammates, trainers, and even his catchers, those who had shared the weight of 100 mph fastballs and milestone moments. The crowd roared with every mention of his storied journey.

That day was more than a ceremony it was a celebration of everything Nolan Ryan had come to represent: power, perseverance, class, and an unwavering love for the game. His bronze plaque now rests in Cooperstown, but his legend continues to echo in every batter who swings late on a fastball and in every pitcher who dares to chase greatness.

Conclusion

To wrap this up, let's channel that golden-era sportscaster. Imagine the grainy crackle of an old broadcast, maybe a pipe in the background, and a voice like Vin Scully or Howard Cosell delivering this with flair and reverence.

"Ladies and gentlemen, as we wind down the remarkable tale of Nolan Ryan, yes, the Nolan Ryan you must remember: this wasn't just the story of one man and his thunderbolt right arm. No, sir. This was baseball, in all its glory, a rich, colorful tapestry, woven from the sweat and spirit of legends past and present.

From his first victim, Pat Jarvis, to his final punch-out, Greg Myers, Nolan Ryan didn't just pitch; he performed. He was the headliner, sure, but the show? The show was shared. Every batter, every catcher, every teammate and coach played a role in a drama that stretched across four decades of hardball history.

And oh, the legends he faced! Aaron, Brett, Yastrzemski, Reggie, Henderson! If they've got a plaque in Cooperstown, there's a good chance Nolan Ryan faced 'em down and sent 'em back to the dugout wondering what just blew past.

The Hall of Fame might as well have its own wing for men who once stood helplessly against the Ryan Express.

But in the end, this saga ain't just about Ks and no-nos. It's about connection. It's about continuity. It's about a game passed down like a family heirloom from generation to generation, from mound to batter's box. Nolan Ryan didn't just leave a mark, he carved a legend into the very grain of the game.

So as we pack up our scorebooks and tip our caps to Number 34, let's remember: this wasn't a solo act. This was baseball. Pure, shared, and eternal. And no one did it quite like Nolan Ryan."

The Author

For many years, I hardly thought about baseball cards at all.

Every once in a while, I would stumble across my small childhood collection — fewer than twenty cards, tucked away since middle school in the early 1990s. Most of them featured Nolan Ryan, alongside a handful of other players we once believed would someday be valuable. Like any careful young collector, I had stored them in top loaders and placed them in a small card box that eventually traveled from state to state, house to house, and closet to closet for more than three decades, quietly collecting dust.

Until recently.

One evening, I found myself sitting on the bed with my 13-year-old daughter, helping her sleeve and organize her Pokémon cards into a new binder. As I offered advice on protecting her collection, something stirred — a familiar feeling I hadn't expected to return. Memories of childhood collecting resurfaced, and before long, I found myself diving headfirst back into the hobby.

Down the rabbit hole we go.

As I began researching modern cards, I quickly realized that while they are visually stunning, they weren't what I was drawn to. I wanted something familiar. Something meaningful. Something rooted in history.

Nolan Ryan felt like the natural place to begin — after all, I already had a few of his cards waiting.

When I commit to a project, I tend to go deep — sometimes before fully understanding what I'm getting into. I soon discovered that many collectors pursue complete career runs of Ryan's playing years, from 1968 through 1994. That sounded like a worthy challenge. I located what I believed was a comprehensive checklist of his cards, only to find an overwhelming list spanning every brand ever produced. One detail stood out: Topps was the only company to issue cards covering his entire career. That became my starting point.

I set out to complete a Topps master run.

At first, the list seemed manageable — roughly 120 cards. Doable, I thought. Only later did I come to understand the scarcity, cost, and complexity of many of those issues. But by then, I was committed.

That commitment led me into a deep and rewarding rabbit hole — one I still suspect has no true bottom.

At the time of this writing, my checklist has grown to more than 350 cards, and I've completed over 80 percent of it. The journey has been fascinating, but at some point, I realized I wanted more than a chronological run of cardboard. I wanted a collection with narrative meaning — something that captured *the story* of Nolan Ryan, not just the years he played.

That curiosity led me to Ryan's records.

Collecting every player involved in his seven no-hitters felt too vast, so I began looking elsewhere — toward his strikeout milestones. Ryan recorded 5,714 strikeouts, and within that number were moments of history: the hitters who became the 1,000th, 2,000th, 3,000th, and even the 5,000th victim — including legends like Rickey Henderson.

Ryan was the force behind those numbers, but he never stood alone. His legacy was shaped not only by his dominance, but by the players he faced, the teammates who supported him, and the people who influenced or were influenced by his career.

From that realization, a new collection was born — a signed micro-collection built around three guiding ideas:

1. Players directly tied to Ryan's milestones
2. People who significantly impacted his career
3. Individuals connected to compelling or meaningful Ryan-related stories

I wanted the collection to *tell a story*. Not just for collectors — but for someone unfamiliar with Ryan's dominance, someone who could walk through the cards and understand *why each player mattered* without needing a lengthy explanation.

Collectors may be familiar with the Pacific *Texas Express* sets, which chronicle Ryan's milestones through cards centered on him. My approach took a different path. Rather than spotlighting Ryan alone, I chose to spotlight the *people connected to his moments.*

To do this, I created custom one-paragraph story cards to accompany each player — short narrative snapshots that explain their connection to Ryan and the significance of the moment they shared. As part of the creative process, I used ChatGPT to help test ideas, verify details, and experiment with storytelling. The use of AI became an unexpectedly enjoyable tool, and I learned a great deal along the way.

As the collection grew, so did the scope of the project. I found myself wanting to understand the deeper context behind each milestone, each opponent, and each defining moment. One evening, while discussing the project with a fellow Nolan Ryan collector, he remarked that the concept felt less like a collection — and more like the foundation of a book.

And so, here we are.

This book exists to explore the people and players who shaped Nolan Ryan's career — from historic strikeout victims to teammates, rivals, and figures who helped define the legend on and off the field.

Writing it has been one of the most rewarding projects of my life. Beyond research and storytelling, I reached out to many of the players featured in these pages. I had the privilege of interviewing several of them and receiving letters from others. All direct player quotes included in this book come from those personal conversations and correspondence.

In many ways, this book — like the collection that inspired it — is not just about Nolan Ryan.

It is about the people who stood across from him, beside him, and within the moments that built his legend.

A Note on the Writing Process: I am not a novelist by trade; I'm a software engineer and a baseball card collector, and a man who loves both the rhythm of baseball and the hum of technology. To shape my thoughts into story, I turned to modern tools, AI among them, to help translate research into rhythm and outline into prose. But every chapter, every fact, every line of intent was guided and edited by me. The machine offered structure; the heart, the meaning, and the obsession, those are entirely human.

This book is the product of that partnership: curiosity and code, memory and machine, bound together in service of a single purpose to tell Nolan Ryan's story, and the stories of those who shared the field with him.

I hope you enjoy reading it as much as I loved creating it.

Notes & Sources

Many of the stories in *The K Chronicles* were built on firsthand accounts, letters, interviews, and memories generously shared by players, umpires, fans, and collectors. While the narratives in this book are carefully edited for clarity and flow, I believe in preserving the full context of those conversations.

To that end, selected raw interview transcripts, extended responses, and supplemental research materials are available on the book's companion website: www.TheKChronicles.com.

There, you'll find original quotes in full, bonus content that didn't make it into print, and additional resources for anyone looking to dig deeper into the people and history behind Nolan Ryan's remarkable career. Whether you're a fellow collector, a baseball historian, or just curious about the process, I hope the archive adds to your experience.

Primary Sources

Arnsberg, Brad. *Letter to the author.* June 2025.

Berry, Ken. *Interview with the author.* May 2025.

Clouston, Bob. *Letter to the author.* July 2025.

Dawson, Andre. *Interview with the author.* May 2025.

Garcia, Rich. *Interview with the author.* June 2025.

Howe, Art. *Interview with the author.* July 2025.

Jarvis, Pat. *Letter to the author.* May 2025.

Krick, Steve. *Letter to the author.* July 2025.

McCreary, Walt. *Interview with the author.* July 2025.

Meoli, Rudy. *Email to the author.* May 2025.

Mills, Brad. *Interview with the author. October 2025.*

Morganna, Roberts ("the Kissing Bandit"). *Letter to the author.* June 2025.

Secondary Sources

"Alan Ashby." *SABR BioProject*, edited by Bill Nowlin, Society for American Baseball Research https://sabr.org/bioproj/person/alan-ashby/

"Norm Cash." *SABR BioProject*, Society for American Baseball Research https://sabr.org/bioproj/person/norm-cash/

"Red Murff." *SABR BioProject*, Society for American Baseball Research https://sabr.org/bioproj/person/red-murff/

"Jeff Torborg." *SABR BioProject*, Society for American Baseball Research https://sabr.org/bioproj/person/jeff-torborg/

Detroit Free Press. "Cash Swings Table Leg After Running Out of Bats." *Detroit Free Press*, 16 July 1973, p. C1.

Houston Astros. *Houston Astros Media Guide.* 1987 edition.

Retrosheet. "Box Score and Play-by-Play, May 15, 1973: California Angels at Kansas City Royals." *Retrosheet* https://www.retrosheet.org/boxesetc/1973/B05150KCA1973.htm

Retrosheet. “Box Score and Play-by-Play, Oct 14, 1969: New York Mets vs. Baltimore Orioles, World Series Game 3.” *Retrosheet* https://www.retrosheet.org/boxesetc/1969/B10140NYN1969.htm

General Statistical References

Baseball-Reference.com. “Nolan Ryan Statistics and History.” *Baseball Reference*, Sports Reference LLC https://www.baseball-reference.com/players/r/ryanno01.shtml

Baseball-Reference.com. “1969 World Series Game 3, Box Score and Play-by-Play.” *Baseball Reference* https://www.baseball-reference.com/boxes/NYN/NYN196910140.shtml

Retrosheet. “Nolan Ryan Game Logs and Play-by-Play Data.” *Retrosheet* https://www.retrosheet.org/boxesetc/R/Pryann001.htm

Collector's Checklist

If you've found your way here, chances are you collect baseball cards—and there's a good chance Nolan Ryan has a place in your binders, boxes, or display cases.

This book was born from that same impulse. What began as a personal collecting journey—centered on Ryan's cards—soon grew into something more: a deeper exploration of the players who crossed paths with him at pivotal moments. Strikeouts, no-hitters, bench-clearing brawls, rookie debuts, and final farewells—each chapter traces one of those intersections.

If you're looking to build a collection that echoes the stories in these pages, I've included a full checklist of every player featured in the book.

A more detailed and downloadable version is available on the website.

Part 1: Origins	
	Red Murff
	Tom Seaver
	Jerry Koosman

Part 2: Milestone Strikeouts	
	Pat Jarvis (First Strikeout)
	Sal Bando (1,000 Strikeout)
	Ron LeFlore (2,000 Strikeout)
	Cesar Geronimo (3,000 Strikeout)
	Brad Mills (3,509 Strikeout)
	Danny Heep (4,000 Strikeout)
	Rickey Henderson (5,000 Strikeout)
	Greg Myers (5,714 Strikeout)

Part 3: Record-Breaking Moments	
	Jeff Torborg
	Rudy Meoli
	Rich Reese
	Norm Cash
	Gaylord Perry
	Steve Carlton
	Art Howe
	Ruben Sierra
	Alan Ashby
	Brad Arnsberg

Part 4: Power vs Power	
	Carl Yastrzemski
	Roger Maris
	Mark McGwire
	Barry Bonds
	Pete Rose
	Andre Dawson
	Will Clark

Part 5: Fights, Ejections, and Flashpoints	
	Bo Jackson
	Rich Garcia
	Willie Wilson
	Robin Ventura
	Morganna

Part 6: Behind the Legend	
	Bobby Valentine
	Tom House

Part 7: Generations & Lineages	
	Dick Schofield Sr.
	Dick Schofield Jr.
	Tito Francona
	Terry Francona
	Maury Wills
	Bump Wills
	Hal McRae
	Brian McRae
	Ken Griffey Sr.
	Ken Griffey Jr.
	Bobby Bonds
	Barry Bonds
	Sandy Alomar Sr.
	Sandy Alomar Jr.
	Roberto Alomar

** Part 8 omitted intentionally*

Part 9: Legacy & Farewell	
	Randy Johnson

www.ingramcontent.com/pod-product-compliance
Lightning Source LLC
LaVergne TN
LVHW010902110826
845149LV00005B/1445

9798994845202